Hawaiian Home Cookin'

Written and Illustrated by
Mama Annie

Graphics by Surya Burdick

ISBN# 0-9637637-8-4
© copyright 2002 by Cleall Publishing
13920 Green Valley Rd.
Forestville, Ca. 95436

INTRODUCTION AND ACKNOWLEDGEMENTS

The cooking in Hawaii and in all the Pacific Islands, as cooking all over the world, is based on what grows in the region. Thus, fish and fruit are common. Lush trees and plants produce tastes such as ginger, tamarind, galangal and lemon grass. Apples, pears, and other plants that need a dormant season are less common in the islands. So when in the islands, I cook like the islanders do and take what I've learned home with me.

There are many influences in the cuisine of Hawaii, among them, Asian, Indonesian and Portuguese . In this book I will present menus using spices and flavors from all over the South Pacific. These are becoming more and more available in special-ty stores everywhere. There are traditional recipes and revised recipes. For instance, the Hawaiians cook fish, pork and/or chicken wrapped in taro, ti and banana leaves. When I'm not in the islands, I live in the wine country. Banana leaves and ti leaves are difficult to find. So, I wrap my fish, not mahi-mahi or opah, but ling cod or salmon, in grape leaves. In the islands I garnish my plates with star fruit and orchids, in California I use blackberries and nasturtium blossoms. Much of my culinary cre-ativity is prompted by laziness. I would much rather invent some-thing new than go to the store to get something I forgot.

I hope this book will encourage you to mix regional and ethnic flavors. I have certainly created some odd dishes doing this but, all in all, it's a fun and rewarding practice. Adventure in cooking is as exciting as adventure where ever you find it.

I wish to thank those of you who loaned me very old Hawaiian cookbooks, who gave me your favorite island recipes and who helped with the research, Cousin Julie who helped open Mama's Fishhouse on Maui, Kathi and Jenni, David and Dennis, sister Deb, Lolo and Sama Mataafa and his mother, and Barbara on Molokai.

Mama Annie

STORIES AND LEGENDS

Many of the recipes in this book have small time gaps, as in, "add the carrots, cook three minutes , then add the nuts and parsley." I have found that I'm inclined to leave the kitchen for these three minutes. This often spells disaster. I answer the phone or pick up the mail and soon there is smoke pouring from the kitchen. To prevent this problem in like minded people, I have included some light reading material to pass the three or five minute intervals herein. The Polynesian culture abounds in legends. They weave in and out of the history like a metallic thread in a woven homespun shawl. Most legends have a myriad of versions and any one may vary from island to island. I have selected a few of my favorites and condensed them down to the three minute format. I intend this as light entertainment, but also as a taste of some very rich reading if you care to look further. I sincerely hope that in condensing these stories, I did not misinterpret them. My apologies to any and all Kahunas for any mistakes.

TABLE OF CONTENTS

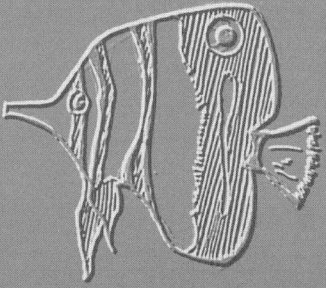
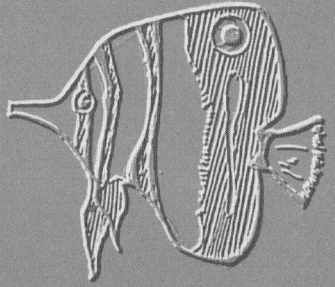

Breakfasts

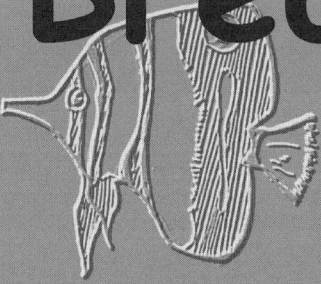
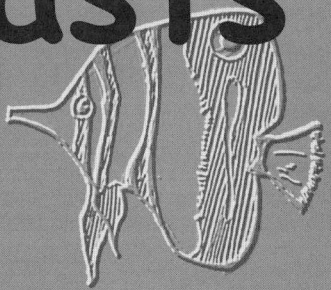

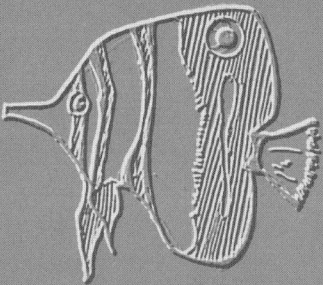
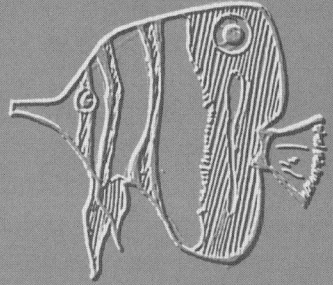

CLASSIC LOCO MOCO

Almost any "local" restaurant and some of the newer 'chic' restaurants, will have "loco moco" on the breakfast menu. I will start with the classic one and then include a few variations.

1 pound hamburger
4 cups cooked white rice
1 tablespoon butter
4 eggs
1 can brown gravy or homemade brown gravy

Divide hamburger meat into 4 flat patties, ½ inch thick and cook through, about 3 minutes per side. Heat gravy. Heat rice. Melt butter in skillet and fry eggs, turning once. Mound 1 cup rice on each plate, top with hamburger, then egg, and pour the gravy over all.

Homemade Gravy

1 heaping tablespoon butter
2 tablespoons flour
1 can beef broth
1 onion, sliced thin, sautéed in
1 Tablespoon each, butter and cooking oil.
Salt and Pepper

On low heat, melt butter, Add flour and stir into butter. Cook, stirring constantly for 1 minute. Slowly add ½ the can of broth, stirring quickly with a whisk to eliminate lumps. Be patient. If you just keep stirring, squishing lumps, it will eventually get smooth. Add more broth until you like the consistency. You will want it the thickness of syrup. Add onions if you are using them and salt and pepper to taste.

This serves 4 or 2 really hungry guys

LOCO MOCO WITH FISH

4 cups cooked white rice
4 pieces fish, ahi, ono or mahi work well
3 tablespoons butter
4 eggs
Gravy with soy sauce (recipe below)

Over medium heat, pan fry fish in 2 tablespoon of the butter 3 to 4 minutes per side for ½ inch thickness. Flake a section to see if shininess has gone. It should be opaque and flaky all the way through. It is easy to over cook and not nearly as delicious so don't cook it for 10 minutes, just to 'be sure'. Melt remaining butter in skillet and fry eggs, turning once. Mound 1 cup rice on each of 4 plates. Top with 1 piece of fish, then 1 egg and cover each with gravy.

Gravy with soy sauce

1 can chicken broth
1 ¼ tablespoon corn starch
1 tablespoon soy sauce
1 tablespoon butter (optional)
Salt and Pepper

Put ¾ cup chicken broth in small pan. Stir in cornstarch until dissolved. I leat over low to medium heat until thickened. Add more broth if it gets too thick. Stir in soy sauce and taste. Add salt if necessary and pepper to taste. Add and stir in butter if you want a richer gravy.

Serves 4

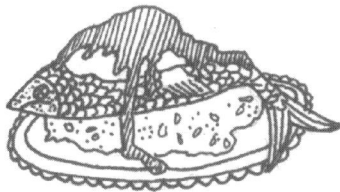

EGG FOO YUNG LOCO MOCO

This one got so creative, I'm not even sure it qualifies as a Loco Moco but it sure is good.

8 egg foo yung (recipe below)
6 cups cooked white rice
8 thin slices ham
1 can chicken gravy*

Make egg foo yung, keep hot. Heat gravy. Heat ham slices in oven or fry quickly. Mound 1 cup rice on each of 4 plates. Top with 1 slice ham, then 1 egg foo yung, then ½ cup rice, then 1 more slice ham and 1 more egg foo yung, and finally top with gravy.

Egg Foo Yung

6 eggs
1 ½ tablespoons soy sauce
2 scallions, finely chopped
4 large mushrooms, finely chopped
1 cup bean sprouts
3 tablespoons butter

Lightly beat eggs with soy sauce. Add scallions, mushrooms and bean sprouts. Melt butter in skillet, a little at a time as you need it. Pour or spoon in batter as you would for pancakes, making each omelet 4 to 5 inches in diameter. You should end up with 8 of them. Keep warm while assembling the dish.

This will feed 4 hungry people. If you have lightweights, give them 1 slice ham and one egg foo yung.

*The gravy with soy sauce used with the fish Loco Moco works well with this too.

SPAM LOCO MOCO

4 slices Spam
4 slices pineapple
4 cups cooked white rice
4 green onions
4 poached or fried eggs
1 tablespoon cooking oil
1 can chicken gravy
2 tablespoons Asian plum sauce (optional)

Heat gravy. Using only the green part, chop the onions. Sauté onions in 1 tablespoon cooking oil 3 or 4 minutes, until limp. Remove from pan and keep warm. Add Spam to pan and sauté until slightly browned on both sides. Remove from pan and keep warm. Add a little more oil if needed. Add pineapple slices to pan and sauté until slightly browned on both sides. Heat the rice if it's cold. Stir green onions into rice. Mound 1 cup rice on each of 4 plates. Place 1 pineapple slice on each mound and a slice of Spam on the pineapple and an egg on top of the Spam. Top with hot gravy. To finish this dish, I like to drizzle a little plum sauce over the top. Plum jam or any other jam may work well too.

Serves 4

MACADAMIA NUT PANCAKES

¾ cups milk, low-fat is fine
2 tablespoons melted butter
1 egg
1 cup all-purpose flour
2 teaspoons baking powder
4 tablespoons sugar
1 teaspoon vanilla
½ cup coarsely chopped macadamia nuts

Beat the milk, butter, and egg, lightly. Add vanilla. Mix the dry ingredients and add to the milk mixture. Stir just enough to combine. Fold in nuts. Lightly oil a griddle or frying pan and heat to medium hot. Drop batter by spoonfuls and cook until bubbles form on the top. Flip cakes and brown the other side. I like these with coconut syrup. If you're feeling lazy, you can mix up a commercial pancake mix. Then add a little sugar, the vanilla, and the macadamia nuts.

Makes 10 or 12 pancakes

RICE SCRAMBLE

½ cup ham, spam, or cooked pork, diced small
½ cup diced onion
¼ cup diced celery
¼ cup diced red and/or green pepper
1 tablespoon oil
1 cup cooked white rice
6 eggs, beaten
2 tablespoons parmesan or jack cheese
salt and pepper, to taste

Stir fry onion, celery and red and green pepper in oil for 2 minutes, add meat and stir 1 more minute. Stir in rice and combine. Stir in eggs and cook until just set. Sprinkle cheese on top and put under broiler for 2 minutes or until cheese melts and top is cooked. Add salt and pepper to your taste. I like this with flour tortillas but with the rice, it's very filling on it's own.

Serves 3 or 4.

SPAM BREAKFAST FRITTERS

These little guys are really good. I like them with hot, pure maple syrup.

1 cup water
½ cup butter, cut in pieces
¼ teaspoon salt
1 cup all-purpose flour
4 eggs
¼ cup diced Spam, or ham
¼ cup corn kernels
1 tablespoon minced chives
oil for frying

Bring the cup of water to a boil in a 2 quart pan. Add the butter and salt and stir until the butter melts. Remove from heat and dump in flour all at once. Stir vigorously until it forms a ball. Add the eggs, one at a time, beating vigorously after each one. Now fold* in the Spam, corn and chives. Drop by tablespoonful into hot oil and cook in batches, until brown. Remove from oil and drain on paper towels.

One of my kids called me, while trying to follow one of my recipes, and asked "What does 'fold' mean?" To fold is to gently turn the batter over until new ingredient is incorporated. A rubber spatula is my tool of choice for this job.

Makes about 12 fritters.

PEANUT BUTTER BANANA TOAST

There are those of us who just want bread for breakfast. Really good toast, French toast, or sweet breads. Here is my all time favorite. My girlfriend and I used to get up very early, jump in the ocean with our little paddle boards (neither one of us swim very well), and head for the snorkeling spot. There we would lay, one hand on the board, and watch fish for an hour, often two. Then we would paddle the half mile or so back, and race home to make the following breakfast.

4 pieces heavy whole wheat bread
4 apple bananas
¼ jar chunky peanut butter
honey

Toast the bread. Spread generously with peanut butter. Slice one apple banana on each piece of toast. Drizzle on lots of honey. Mmmmm-mmmm.

Serves about 2.

FRENCH TOAST SANDWICH

8 slices bread, your choice, sliced fairly thin
soft butter
4 apple bananas, or 2 large bananas
Guava jelly
3 large eggs
dash cinnamon, (optional)
oil for frying

Lightly butter bread. Spread a layer of guava jelly on each of the pieces. Slice bananas on top of the jelly on 4 of the pieces. Top with the other 4 pieces making 4 sandwiches. Beat eggs and add the dash of cinnamon if desired. Dip sandwiches in egg on both sides and fry until lightly browned on both sides. Serve with syrup or dusted with powdered sugar.

Makes 4 sandwiches.

PAPAYA

Papaya is a very common sight on breakfast tables in Hawaii. It is light and delicious and contains an enzyme called papain, which is a natural aid to digestion. It is most often cut in half and seeded and served with a lime to squeeze over it. Here are a few other suggestions, including one I came up with that is very popular with my friends and family.

Papaya with yoghurt. Halve and seed a papaya and fill cavity with your favorite fruit yoghurt, or plain yoghurt with mango chunks on top.

Fill cavity of halved papaya with cottage cheese and top with chopped macadamia nuts. .

And my favorite!

1 papaya, halved and seeded
1 ripe nectarine
1 banana
¼ cup grated coconut

Chop nectarine and banana into bite sized pieces and mix them together. Fill cavity of papayas with fruit pieces. Toast coconut in frying pan. When coconut is brown and hot (usually not more than 1 minute) divide it over the chopped fruit on the papaya halves. The combination of the hot coconut and the cold fruit is delightful, but if you have to make them ahead and the coconut cools, it's still very delicious.

Serves 2

LONG RICE OMELET

This is a fun and different omelet. It tastes a little like egg-foo-yung. Long rice is cellophane noodles, which are made from rice flour.

¼ cup green onions, chopped
¼ cup slivered ham or Spam
2 tablespoons chopped red bell pepper
1 tablespoon oil
1 cup long rice
4 or 5 eggs
salt and pepper

Put long rice in a deep bowl and cover with boiling water. Allow to sit for 20 minutes or so until tender. Sauté onions, ham, and red pepper in oil, on low heat, for 4 to 5 minutes, until softened. Beat eggs and add a pinch of salt. Drain long rice, cut in pieces and add to eggs. Pour this mixture over ham and vegetables in sauté pan and cook over low heat. When starting to firm, turn the omelet and cook the other side 1 minute or so. Add salt and pepper to taste.

Serves 2, or 4 as a side dish

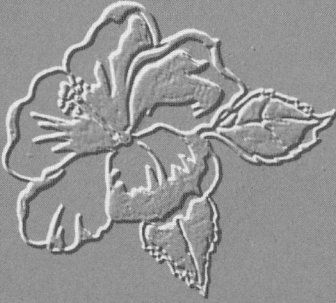
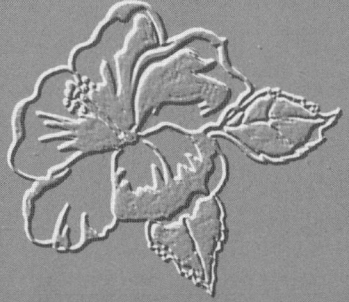

Appetizers

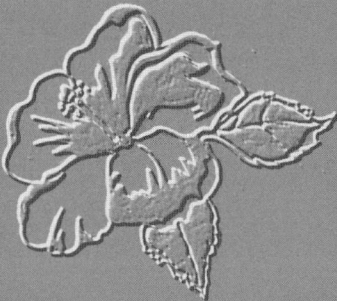
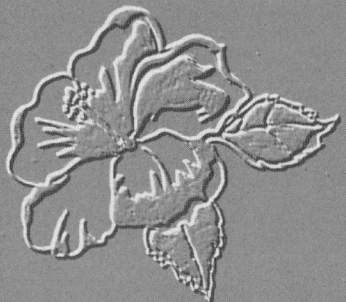

SPAM ENVELOPES

We can't talk about Hawaiian country cooking without talking about Spam. You will see it dispersed liberally throughout the recipes in this book, as it is as common as fish in Hawaii. I am always amazed at the creative ways people have of using it. Here is one of my favorite concoctions.

1 cup Chinese cabbage or bok choy, finely chopped
½ cup chives, finely chopped
2 cloves garlic, finely chopped
¾ cup finely chopped Spam
2 tablespoons cilantro leaves, finely chopped
¼ tsp. salt and a dash of pepper
1 egg yolk, lightly beaten
8 large flour tortillas
4 tablespoons canola oil

Mix 1st 6 ingredients in a large bowl. Lay out 4 of the tortillas and divide mixture among them, spreading to within 1 inch from the edge. With a pastry brush or finger, coat the edges with the egg yolk. Press remaining 4 tortillas on the top of each one with the spam mixture and seal the edges. Allow to sit while you heat oil in skillet, then quickly brown each of them on both sides. Drain on paper towels and cut into 4 pieces. Serve these as an appetizer or 4 pieces to a person for a lunch, or two pieces, accompanied by fish, salad, or whatever, for dinner.

HAIKU ROLLS

An island version of a California roll.

2 cups cooked sushi rice
1 or 2 mangos, cut small to equal 1 cup
2 rounded tablespoons water chestnut or Daikon radish, minced
2 tablespoons Asian Plum Sauce
2 sheets nori*
About 10 medium shrimp, cooked
2 tablespoons peanut or vegetable oil
½ teaspoon sesame oil
1 teaspoon soy sauce
1 teaspoon rice vinegar
½ teaspoon sugar

Combine oils, soy sauce, vinegar and sugar. Toss cooked shrimp in this mixture and allow to marinate. Lay nori on flat working surface. Cover with rice ¼ inch thick, leaving ¼ inch borders on three sides and 1 inch border on one side. Mix mango pieces with chestnut or radish pieces and the Plum Sauce. Spoon ½ of mixture down the middle of the rice on a parallel with the 1 inch border. Using a bamboo roller, or your hands, roll the nori tightly toward the 1 inch border. Wet the 1 inch border and seal the roll. Refrigerate if you have the time, to make cutting easier. With a very sharp knife cut roll into discs 1 inch or so thick. Tuck a shrimp, tail up, into the center of each and serve.

* Nori is the black seaweed used to make sushi rolls. It is available in most supermarkets and all Asian markets.

PELE

The most feared and revered figure in the vast pantheon of Polynesian Goddesses and demi-Gods, is without question, Pele. She is the fire-Goddess who presides over the lava flow. Pele is beautiful and magnificent, ferocious and terrible, transforms often into fire, lava flow, a beautiful young maiden, an old woman or a white dog. She lives with family members at the volcano at Kilauea. Hi'iaka, the younger sister and favorite sibling of Pele, is the supreme patroness of the hula. One of the most well-known Pele myths revolves around her and Hi'iaka.

Pele arrives on the island of Kauai where there is a hula dance in progress. She assumes the form of a beautiful maiden. Her beauty and her dancing capture the heart of the young chief, Lohiau, and they are wed. After three days of honeymoon, Pele leaves the island to find a home for the two of them and promises to send a messenger for him when she has settled. Upon finding their home, she entrusts the mission to her younger sister Hi'iaka who is the only one brave enough to volunteer. She asks for and is given Goddess power and, with women friends, embarks on her journey, leaving her beloved lehua groves and her friend Hopoe in the care of Pele. She is immediately beset with horrendous obstacles, the first being the evil mo'o people, several of whom she turns into lava rock. They are followed by the shark at the mouth of Waipio valley, the prudish ghost god who punished girls for swimming nude across the stream holding their clothes above their heads, and countless others. They finally arrive on Kauai to find that Lohiau has died, mourning the loss of his beautiful bride. But, no problem, Hi'iaka finds his body hidden in a cave, catches his fluttering spirit, and restores it to the body. Meanwhile the forty days allotted to the journey are long gone and Pele is beginning to blow smoke out of her nostrils. At sea, the shark gods and the sea goddess, who are kin of Pele, are doing their best to prevent Hi'iaka from delivering a mere mortal to be the husband of their divine relative. As they pass Oahu, Hi'iaka stops to climb a cliff to look toward her home on Hawaii, only to see her sister has set fire to her lehua groves and has surrounded her dear friend, Hopoe, in lava.

In spite of her sister's betrayal, Hi'iaka sends her two friends ahead to explain their delay, but Pele is in such a jealous rage, she consumes them in fire before they can speak. At this, Hi'iaka in full view of her sister, embraces Lohiau. Pele encircles them in flame. Hi'iaka, a divinity, cannot be harmed but Lohiau dies again, but again, no problem. As these tales go on forever, I will now encourage you to purchase one of the many books on Hawaiian myths and see what happened.

FINGER-LICKIN' CHICKEN FINGERS

A crispy, nummy appetizer, they might be good in a sandwich too.

2 skinless, boneless, chicken breasts
½ cup sweet and hot mustard
¾ cup breadcrumbs or panko*
oil for frying
salt
4 cloves garlic
½ cup mayonnaise thinned with 2 tablespoons milk
Or ½ cup ranch dressing

Cut chicken breasts in ¼ inch strips to form "fingers". Coat fingers with mustard, then dip in breadcrumbs, coating well. Heat oil to medium hot and quickly fry chicken fingers, not more than 1 to 1 ½ minutes per side. Drain on paper towels. Sprinkle with salt if needed. Mince, then mash garlic and add to mayonnaise for a dip, or dip into ranch dressing.

* Panko is an Asian version of breadcrumbs which is light and fries well.

PORK AND HAM MEATBALLS

These taste unlike any meatballs you've ever had. I used to make them with ground ham but found minced ham gives them a different and delightful texture. You can also cook this in a loaf pan. I slice this thin and serve it with eggs for breakfast or in sandwiches. Sometimes I serve the meatballs over rice with a gravy made of pan drippings. I'm including a recipe for a dipping sauce to serve with the meatballs as an appetizer.

1 pound ground pork
1 pound cooked ham cut in ¼ inch cubes
1 cup breadcrumbs
1 onion, chopped
2 eggs
½ teaspoon ground sage
2 dashes ground rosemary
2 tablespoons oil for frying

Combine all ingredients except oil. Form meat mixture into walnut size balls and cook in oil, over medium heat until browned on all sides and cooked through, approximately 10 minutes. Serve with dipping sauce. Alternately, put meat mixture in a loaf pan and bake at 325 degrees for 1 ½ hours.

Dipping sauce

1/3 cup brown sugar
1 tablespoon dry mustard
¼ cup apple cider vinegar
½ cup catsup

Put all ingredients in a small saucepan and cook over low heat until combined and heated.

SPICY MISO CLAMS

Clams in a butter, wine, and garlic sauce are hard to beat but my family and I really enjoy this clam recipe for a change.

2 pounds clams
3 large cloves garlic
4 large shallots or 1 small onion
2 tablespoons grated ginger
1 heaping tablespoon yellow bean paste (miso)*
½ to 1 teaspoon hot pepper paste*
½ teaspoon sugar
3 tablespoons cooking oil
2 green onions

Scrub clams. Chop shallot or onion, mince garlic and grate ginger. Heat oil and saute onion, garlic, and ginger for 1 minute. Add clams and stir to coat with oil. Add miso, pepper paste, sugar and ¼ cup of water. Stir to combine and cover. Cook for 2 to 5 minutes, depending on size of clams. Chop and add the green onions for the last 30 seconds of cooking. Discard any clams that don't open.

These are available in Asian markets. There is a red miso that would work but I don't find it quite as flavorful.

COCONUT RICE LOLIPOPS

This is a delicacy from the Phillipines. It is slightly sweet and can be served as a dessert, but also fits very nicely on an appetizer buffet.

1 cup medium grain rice
1 cup coconut milk
¼ cup sugar
1 egg
1 tablespoon lemon juice
1 cup shredded coconut
oil for frying
powdered sugar
toothpicks

Cook rice in 1 cup water and 1 cup coconut milk, until very soft. Cool and add the egg, sugar and lemon juice. Wet your hands and roll rice into small balls and then into the shredded coconut to coat. Fry a few at a time until coconut browns. Transfer to a plate and dust with powdered sugar. Put a toothpick in each of them.

SPAM POPS

My brother called these Spam Pops and gave them an A+.
They're different and fun! They're also easy to put together and
with a little care, not hard to cook. I'm giving you two versions.

1 + ½ cups cooked sushi rice*
2 ¾ inch slices of Spam
¼ cup sesame seeds
1 green onion
oil for frying
Sauces

First version: Cut Spam into cubes ½ to ¾ inches square. Wet
your hands and put 2 tablespoonsful of rice into your palm.
Place a cube of Spam in the center and form rice around it into a
ball about the size of a ping pong or a golf ball. Add more rice if
needed. Roll in sesame seeds. Repeat until ingredients are used
up and refrigerate until ready to cook. Heat enough oil in fryer or
saucepan to deep fry and in a fry basket, fry until lightly
browned. You need to handle them gently as they crumble easily. One or two may fall apart, I eat them anyway.

Second version: Chop Spam and green onion into very small
pieces and mix with rice. Form balls and roll in sesame seeds.
Fry as above.

I use the Calrose rice. Most grocery stores have it.

SAUCES

Take ¼ cup good Dijon mustard and mix with water until syrup
thickness. Place 1 or 2 tablespoons on a plate and place 1
Spam Pop on top. Drizzle with Hoisin sauce watered down to
similar consistency.

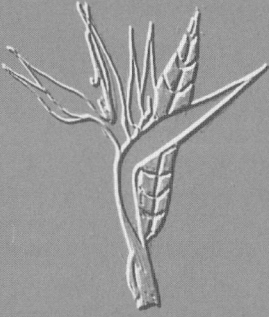

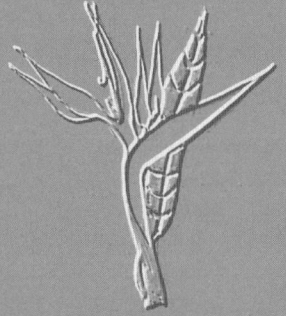

Soups and Salads

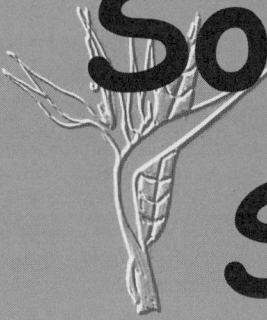

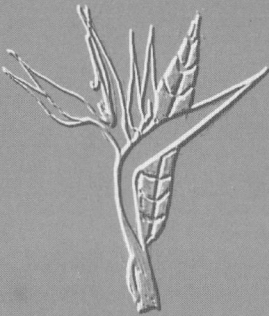

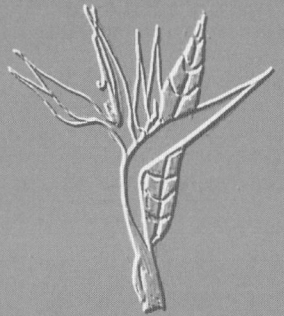

CHICKEN NOODLE SOUP, ISLAND STYLE

This is one of those home style soups like minestrone, in that you can use pretty much whatever's in the refrigerator. I've used spinach and even beet greens in place of the chard. Fresh peas or chinese peas would be good and probably any kinds of mushrooms would work. Sometimes I put fish in it.

BROTH

1 chicken
2 quarts water
1 onion
3 celery tops with leaves*
chicken bouillion granules

Put chicken, water, onion, and celery leaves in a large soup pot and bring to a boil. Turn down and simmer for 1 hour. Remove chicken and vegetables and strain broth. At this point I usually reduce the broth about 1/3, and add some chicken bouillion until it tastes good and chickeny.

I use just the tops of the celery stalks with the leaves for flavoring broths, and save the rest of the stalk for another use.

SOUP

broth
meat from breast and thighs of chicken, cut bite size
4 dried shitake mushrooms
4 fresh white or brown mushrooms
2 stalks lemon grass (optional)
4 slices fresh ginger
1 cup shredded greens (swiss chard, bok choy, etc.)
1 cup bean sprouts
narrow noodles, vermicelli, angel hair etc.
1 teaspoon sesame oil and a few drops chili oil
1 lime

Cut chicken into bite size pieces. 2 breasts is plenty unless you want a lot of meat in it. Soak dried mushrooms in hot water for 20 minutes, then chop, discarding stems. Chop fresh mushrooms and greens. Peel lemon grass, cut into 2 inch lengths and bruise by pressing with a heavy knife. This releases the flavor. You will have only 2 to 4 pieces as most of the stalk is woody and useless. Cut 4 slices fresh ginger. You don't have to peel it. Bring broth to simmer and add, chicken meat, both mushrooms, greens, and sprouts. Lay the ginger and lemon grass on top. Cover and simmer 10 or 15 minutes. Add noodles, I like a bundle with the diameter of a dime but you can use more if you wish. Cook 5 or 6 more minutes.

Now you have to season it to your taste. Squeeze the juice of the lime into it, add the sesame oil and just a few drops of chili oil. Add 1 teaspoon salt. Taste it. If you want it hotter add a few more drops chili oil. You can add more salt, lime juice or sesame oil according to your taste, just do it a little at a time. Remove the lemon grass and the ginger before serving.

Serves 6

STUFFED CABBAGE SOUP

I adapted this from a Japanese recipe. It's a healthy and hearty dish and is very filling.

1 large head cabbage
1 pound sausage, spicy or mild
2 cups cooked white or brown rice
1 onion, minced
1 large clove garlic, minced
3 or 4 mushrooms, minced
2 eggs, lightly beaten
salt and pepper
2 quarts chicken broth, canned is fine
2 tablespoons soy sauce
1 tablespoon rice or white vinegar

Steam cabbage 5 minutes, remove outer leaves and steam 3 to 5 more minutes to soften inner leaves. Take care in removing leaves to keep them whole. Combine sausage, rice, onion, garlic, mushrooms and eggs. Lightly salt and pepper. Lay cooled leaves on flat surface. Place 2 or so tablespoons of sausage mixture on leaf and fold and roll into a little package. I use two of the smaller leaves for a package. Place packages in a steamer over water and steam 45 minutes. Heat broth and season with soy sauce and vinegar. Place cabbage rolls into individual serving bowls and cover with broth.

Serves 6 or more

CARROT COCONUT SOUP

This is a delicious soup, so easy to make. You can sip it from mugs on a picnic or serve it in your finest china to start a meal.

1 onion
2 carrots
1 bay leaf
1 can chicken broth
¾ cup buttermilk
1/3 cup coconut milk(or more to taste)*
½ teaspoon salt

Coarsely chop onion and carrots. Put into a sauce pan with the bay leaf and chicken broth. Simmer for 20 minutes or until vegetables are tender. Remove from heat, cool, put in blender and puree. Add buttermilk and coconut milk. Add salt. Stir and taste. Add more salt if necessary and more coconut milk, a little at a time if you like a stronger coconut taste.

*You can use canned coconut milk or make your own. I have never bought a bad can of coconut milk in Hawaii but on the mainland I've not had such good luck. Most of what we get on the mainland is from Thailand. Some is excellent, but some is tasteless, watery and sometimes even sour. In general, I would avoid the cheaper brands. To make your own, see Coconut Milk in the dessert section.

Serves 4

PAPAYA AVACADO SALAD

Lolo's favorite

1 cup cubed avocado pieces
1 cup cubed strawberry papaya pieces
1 rounded tablespoon chopped mint leaves
2 tablespoons chopped macadamia nuts
salad greens
lime dressing

Combine avocado and papaya pieces with mint leaves. Toss with 1/3 of the dressing. Toss the salad greens with the rest of the dressing. Place greens on 4 plates and top first with papaya mixture and then with the nuts.

Lime dressing

¼ cup canola oil
juice of ½ lime (approximately 1 tablespoon)
1 tablespoon rice vinegar
sea salt to taste.

Combine all ingredients and taste for balance.If it's too tangy, add a little more oil. If it's too bland add a little more salt or vinegar. Serves 4

DAIKON RADISH MANGO SLAW

This is a weird one! A crunchy, juicy, spicy mixture, it pairs very well with grilled fish or chicken, adding a sweet, hot, accent on the side. When I serve it in Sonoma County I call it Banana Slug Slaw, which adds a spark of frivolity to a dinner party, especially if there are 7 to 12 year old boys present. Banana slugs, bless their little hearts, are about as yellow/orange and disgusting looking as it is possible to be.

1 cup coarsely grated daikon radish
1 cup coarsely grated* not quite ripe mango
1/3 cup sour cream
1 tablespoon sugar
1 tablespoon honey
1/4 teaspoon salt

Peel and grate the radish and mango and place in a bowl. Peel the mango thoroughly, as many people are allergic to the skin. Mix the sour cream, sugar, salt, and honey. Mix into the mango and radish, cover with plastic wrap and refrigerate for at least an hour. Taste before serving and add salt if necessary.

*If you find your mango is too ripe for grating, cut it off the pit and then slice it into thin wedges.

Serves 6

MAUI

Maui, in Hawaiian legend, occupies a position much like Coyote in American Indian legend. He is known as the trickster but can also be called upon to perform feats which benefit his people. His mother, Hina, in particular, seems to be always calling on him.

MAUI CAPTURES THE SUN

Hina, the mother of Maui, makes bark cloth, but is unable to dry it in one day. She appeals to Maui to slow down the sun. Maui watches for several days until he knows exactly where the sun will rise. He weaves a cord of coconut fibers and lassos the first rays of the sun as it comes over the horizon. The sun pleads for freedom and after much negotiation, they agree on six months of long days and six months of short days. During all this, Moe Moe is making fun of his effort. When Maui finishes and turns to punish him, he flees. Maui catches up with Moe Moe just north of Lahaina and turns him to stone, where he can be seen today as a long rock beside the road.

While Maui is gone, Hina, who lives near the Wailuku river near Hilo, has a visitor. Kuna, the eel man has come to woo her. She spurns him and he, enraged at the rejection, attempts to drown her. She calls to Maui. He races to her and ensnares Kuna in his sun-catching rope, and turns him into a rock which can still be seen there today. Is it any wonder there are so many rocks on the islands?

BETTA FO' YOU POTATO SALAD

My alpha male food consumer gets very frustrated trying to maintain his boyish figure while eating everything in sight. I concocted this potato salad, keeping the fat count very low, so he could have the best of both worlds.

5 large red skinned potatoes
¾ cup fresh or frozen peas
corn from 1 cob
½ cup chopped lo-fat Spam
½ to ¾ cups lo-fat mayonnaise
1 heaping teaspoon Dijon mustard
1 tablespoon apple cider vinegar
½ to 1 teaspoon salt*
¼ to ½ teaspoon red pepper flakes**

Boil potatoes until tender all the way through and cool completely. Chop into bite-sized pieces. Cook peas until just tender. Scrape kernels off cob of corn and cook until just tender. Put vegetables and Spam a big bowl. Combine remaining ingredients and fold into vegetable mixture. Chill for several hours to combine flavors.

*Start with ½ teaspoon and add until there's enough for your taste. **Adjust this measurement according to how hot you like it. Serves 6 to 8*

ONO NOODLES

This can be used as a salad or a soup. If the weather's blustery I heat it up and call it soup. If it's warm and humid I serve it at room-temperature on lettuce leaves. Ono in the title is the Hawaiian word for delicious.

5 or 6 ounces rice noodles or vermicelli
3 tablespoons vegetable oil
2 teaspoons sesame oil
1 small onion, chopped
2 cloves garlic, minced
2 ½ inch slices Daikon radish, sliced julienne*
8 mushrooms, coarsely chopped
5 dried shitake mushrooms, soaked and coarsely chopped
½ red bell pepper, sliced ¼ inch wide
¼ pound green beans, cut in 2 inch lengths
2 green onions, cut in 1 inch lengths
½ pound shrimp, shelled and deveined
1 to 2 teaspoons curry paste**
2 tablespoons soy sauce
½ cup peanuts

Soak dried mushrooms in a cup of hot water. Cook noodles just until tender and toss in sesame oil. Heat vegetable oil in wok or frying pan. Add onions, radish, and garlic and cook 2 or 3 minutes. Add shitakes, red pepper, beans, cook 2 more minutes. Add shrimp, green onions, curry paste, and soy sauce and cook until heated. Add noodles, toss and serve in bowls or cool and serve on lettuce leaves. Top with peanuts.

*I cut rounds of radish ¼ to ½ inch thick and then slice into strips. **I use a hot madras curry, Your favorite will do nicely. If you use a mild one, you might want to add a couple drops of hot chili oil.*

Serves 4

ORANGE, ASPARAGUS SALAD

This salad is a nice starter for a summer meal. The orange juice dressing is very light and the slightly crunchy asparagus contrasts well with the juicy orange slices.

1 pound asparagus
2 oranges
1 large head red leaf lettuce
2 slices fresh ginger
¼ cup plus 1 tablespoon canola oil
2 tablespoons rice vinegar
4 tablespoons orange juice
1 teaspoon + a dash of soy sauce
¼ to ½ teaspoon salt

Mix canola oil, rice vinegar, orange juice and 1 teaspoon soy sauce. Add salt to taste. Set aside. Slice asparagus on an angle in 1½ inch slices. Discard tough ends. Cut peels off oranges and slice in rounds, then cut rounds in half. Wash lettuce and tear into bite-size pieces. Peel and mince ginger slices. Heat 1 tablespoon oil in saute pan and saute asparagus and ginger for 2 to 3 minutes. Add a dash of soy sauce and cook 1 minute more. Toss lettuce with most of the dressing saving just a little to add to the asparagus and ginger.
Place lettuce on salad plates and top with asparagus mixture and orange slices.

Serves 4

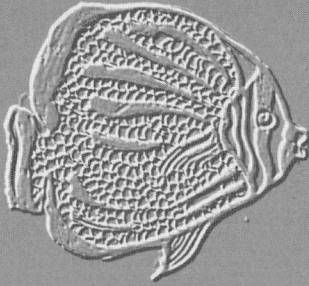
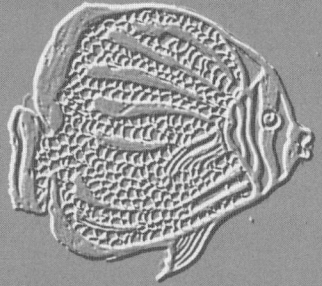

Fish

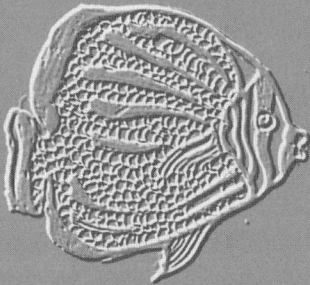
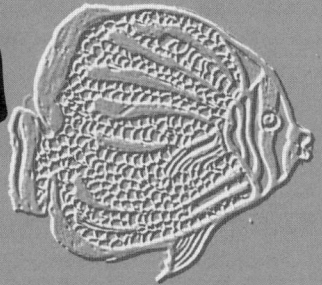

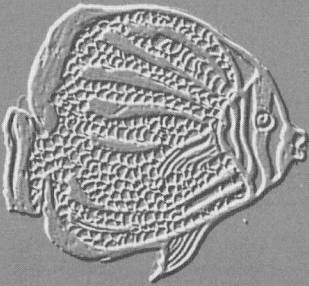
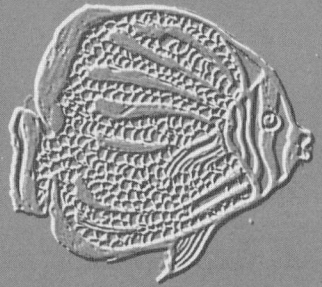

FISH POACHED IN COCONUT MILK

This is a very simple dish. There are so few ingredients that it's important that they all be the best! I serve this fish with white rice mixed with fresh peas and something orange, like mango slices or carrots. The orange stuff is mainly to make the plate look pretty.

2 filets of white fish of your choice
1 tablespoon butter
¾ cup coconut milk
1 teaspoon Hawaiian 'alaea salt, or rock salt

Melt butter in 8 or 9 inch frying pan. Add coconut milk and heat. Add ¼ teaspoon of the salt. Lay fish on milk and cover pan. Cook gently, on medium low heat for 5 minutes or until fish flakes easily in the thickest part. Remove fish to a plate and keep warm. If the juice from the fish has diluted the liquid in the pan, cook over high heat for a minute or two to reduce and thicken sauce. Pour sauce over fish and sprinkle lightly with the lovely coral colored 'alaea salt.

'ALAEA SALT

If you meander around grocery stores in Hawaii, as I do, you
may have seen a little bag of bright coral-colored salt. I bought it
the first time for the color alone, thinking it would look lovely
sprinkled in a soup or on a salad, or in a small dish beside each
plate at a dinner party. It turned out to have a distinctive and
wonderful flavor. Many of the recipes I found from authentic
Hawaiian sources, specifically called for it. It has a soft finish on
the tongue, unlike the biting finish of everyday table salt.

Salt was made in ancient times in the islands, by carving bowls
out of stone, or sometimes wood, and filling them with seawater.
As the water evaporated, it left salt deposits. The salt was then
mixed with 'alaea, or red clay, from the mountains. The stone
carved bowls were often on rocks near the edge of the sea.
Some of the ancient ones can be seen today at Napili Kai on
Maui and in the town of Hanepepe on Kauai. Although until very
recently 'alaea salt was only available to "locals" and their
friends, it is now available in many grocery stores. It can be used
whenever a coarse, Kosher or sea salt is called for.

I have found 'alaea salt makes a wonderful gift for friends who
enjoy cooking. I will often put it into an attractive jar and attach a
little card with the history written on it.

BROILED STICKY SALMON

Sticky salmon may not have been the best name for this. I'm not sure how appetizing that sounds. I know why it's sticky and I know how good it is so it sounds fine to me. We have this dish at least once a week when salmon is fresh and plentiful.

4 salmon filets
½ cup soy sauce
2 tablespoons honey
2 lemon grass stalks, sliced
2 limes or lemons, not both
zest of 2 limes or lemons.

Combine all ingredients except fish in a deep dish. Stir well. If honey is cold, you may have to microwave it for a few seconds in order to integrate it. Dip fish into liquid, turning to coat completely. Allow to marinate in the refrigerator several hours or all day. Line a baking pan or cookie sheet with foil (for easy cleaning). Place fish on foil and broil close to heat, not more than 3 inches from heat source. Fish will get brown and crispy (and a little sticky) on top and be moist inside. A 1 inch cut of fish should take 6 or 8 minutes. I feel very virtuous eating this dish since salmon, along with mackerel and sardines, is being touted as manna for our hearts. In this spirit of healthful eating, I usually serve it with brown rice and stir-fried collard greens.

LOMI LOMI SALMON

Lomi *means massage and lomi-lomi salmon is a bunch of ingredients massaged together. It ends up like a pate' and is a very popular snack or appetizer. Many recipes start with salted salmon but I prefer to get a nice, fresh piece of fish and salt it myself.*

1 pound very fresh salmon filets
Hawaiian 'alaea salt or any coarsely ground salt
4 very ripe, peeled tomatoes
5 or 6 green onions, sliced thin
several drops chili oil

Place raw salmon in a shallow dish and surround it with the salt. Cover and refrigerate over night. Rinse salmon and pat dry. Cut or break into small pieces. Mash tomatoes thoroughly. Add onions and salmon pieces. Mix well. Shake in chili oil, mix again and taste. Add more chili oil if desired. Chill. This is often served on a bed of crushed ice.

SHRIMP CAKES

These can be "messed with". They are like a meat loaf, if you don't have celery, you can use water chestnuts or anything crunchy. You can substitute potato chip crumbs or corn flake crumbs for bread crumbs. I think the texture of the shrimp is essential but if you like, you could mix in some crab or fish with the shrimp.

1 pound bay shrimp or medium shrimp
½ cup homemade breadcrumbs
¼ cup celery, diced small
¼ cup green onions, diced small
½ teaspoon grated fresh ginger root
½ teaspoon salt
1 egg
2 tablespoons mayonnaise
1 teaspoon Dijon mustard
1 package rice noodles or thin egg noodles
3 tablespoons rice flour or corn starch
water
oil for frying

Place shrimp in large bowl. If you have medium shrimp, peel and devein them, and chop into ½ inch pieces. Run 1 or 2 slices of bread through the blender to make crumbs. A heavy wheat bread is very good. Mix egg with mayonnaise and mustard. Combine shrimp, egg mixture, celery, onions, ginger root and salt. Mix well. Form into patties and chill at least ½ hour. Cut noodles into 1 ½ inch lengths and blanch them in very hot water for 5 to 6 minutes. Drain and pat dry, then spread them out on a plate. Mix rice flour or corn starch with enough water to make a thin batter. When shrimp cakes are chilled, dip them in batter then into rice noodles, pressing the noodles on to stick. It's kind of a mess but it's worth it and you can't go too wrong. Fry 2 at a time in oil, at a medium temperature. If the oil is too hot the noodles will brown before the shrimp cake is cooked. 2 minutes on each side should be about right. Serve with plum dipping sauce.Makes 4 cakes.

Plum Dipping Sauce

½ cup sour cream
½ teaspoon chili paste*
2 tablespoons plum sauce*

Mix together.

available in Asian markets and many grocery stores

POACHED FISH WITH VEGETABLES

This poaching liquid is like the French 'court bouillon'. You cook the vegetables in the broth and then steam the fish on top of the vegetables. You can vary the vegetables according to what's available. It's good plain with a little butter melted on the fish but the ginger dressing really makes it extraordinary. I've suggested some fishes, but I think almost any fish would be good.

1 can chicken broth
1 Chinese cabbage, bok choy
4 inches of a daikon radish*
1 large carrot
2 green onions
¼ pound snow peas
2 large or 4 small filets of fish, ono, opah or mahi
salt
Pickled Ginger Dressing

Empty the can of chicken broth into a frying pan and bring to a simmer. Meanwhile cut the radish and carrot into matchstick slices. Cut the green onion into 2 inch lengths and slice long-wise. Clean the snow peas and cut the bok choy into ½ inch strips. Lay the vegetables in the simmering broth, starting with the bok choy. Salt lightly. Cover and cook 3 to 4 minutes. Place fish on top of vegetables and steam 5 to 6 minutes or until fish is done and flakes easily. Lift fish and vegetables onto serving plates and drizzle generously with Pickled Ginger Dressing. This can also be served in a shallow soup bowl utilizing the broth as well.

* Daikon radish is a large, (like a cucumber) white radish. It's a little milder than the small red radishes and provides a nice crispy texture to a dish. It's available in all Asian grocery stores and in many supermarkets.

PICKLED GINGER DRESSING

This dressing is made with Gari which is the pickled ginger you get on a plate of sushi. It is available in jars in the Asian section of most grocery stores. I find this dressing highly versatile. It's very good on fish but just as enhancing to a plate of steamed vegetables or a bowl of white or brown rice.

¼ cup pickled ginger, lightly packed
1 large clove garlic
1 tablespoon soy sauce
1 tablespoon honey
½ teaspoon sesame oil
¼ to ½ teaspoon dried chili peppers
¼ cup canola or other mild oil

Put everything in the blender and blend to a liquid. Scrape down sides once.

SALMON LOAF OR CROQUETTES

This makes a nice luncheon dish and a wonderful appetizer. I make it in small loaf pans and sometimes in mini muffin pans for the appetizer. It's good right out of the oven because it puffs up like a soufflé. It doesn't fall down flat like a soufflé can, so you can also safely refrigerate it for several hours.

1 salmon filet, ½ pound, cooked
½ pound cooked, small or medium shrimp
½ small onion, chopped
1 large garlic clove, cut in 4ths
1 cup cooked rice
1 tablespoon spicy mustard
¼ red bell pepper, cut in 4ths
1 teaspoon prepared wasabi*
¼ teaspoon pepper flakes
½ teaspoon salt
2 eggs

Preheat oven to 400 degrees.
Put everything into a blender or food processor and blend until thoroughly mixed. This can take up to 5 minutes. Spray your loaf pan or muffin tins with cooking oil spray. Spoon the mixture into the pan or tins. You can fill the pans close to the top as it doesn't raise too much. Turn oven down to 375 degrees and bake the loaf for 35 minutes or the muffins for 18 minutes. Slice the loaf and serve either that or the croquettes on lettuce greens, with Hoisin sauce, Plum sauce, or the Pickled Ginger sauce in this book. The loaf can also be served on thin breads or crackers.

Wasabi is the green horseradish you get with sushi. You can buy the prepared paste in a squeeze tube or you can buy it powdered and mix with water. You will want this about the consistency of mustard.

FISH, CHILI, AND REFRIED BEANS

Here's one for Hawaii's many citizens of Mexican heritage.

4 Anaheim chilies
2 red bell peppers
¼ pound jack or feta cheese
2 or 3 tablespoons chopped macadamia or pine nuts
1 large can refried beans
1 pint red salsa, homemade or purchased
5 filets of white fish
½ cup corn meal
½ teaspoon salt
oil for frying

Roast and skin bell peppers, directions below. Cut into ¼ inch strips. Cut Anaheim chilies in half lengthwise. Place in broiler pan. Fill with grated or crumbled cheese. Top with nuts and set aside. Place beans in a microwave safe bowl and soften by mixing in a little water.

Dredge fish filets in corn meal mixed with salt. Fry fish in hot oil, 3 minutes per side for ½ inch filets. Broil Anaheim peppers until cheese is melted and bubbly. Heat beans in microwave. On each of 4 plates, place a portion of beans and cover with salsa. Put 1 piece of fish on beans and salsa and criss-cross the fish with red peppers. Serve the Anaheim peppers on the side.

Roast peppers over direct heat or under broiler, 2 inches below heating element. Turn peppers often until skin is mostly blackened and puckery. Remove peppers to a paper bag. Close and let sweat for 10 minutes. Skins are now easy to peel off.

PEANUT BUTTERFLY SHRIMP

This makes a marvelous appetizer for a fancy party but your family is going to want it for dinner now and then too.

1 pound large or jumbo shrimp
2 teaspoons corn starch
2 tablespoons coconut milk
1 tablespoon peanut butter
1 egg
½ cup almonds, chopped small
½ cup dried, unsweetened coconut
oil for frying
dipping sauce (recipe below)

Shell and butterfly shrimp. Directions on next page. Mix corn starch, coconut milk and peanut butter in medium size bowl. Put shrimp in with this mixture and stir to coat each piece well. Refrigerate for at least half an hour, all day if you want to start early. Just before cooking, beat egg in small bowl and put chopped almonds and coconut each in a small bowl of their own. Dip shrimp, one at a time, into egg, then either into the coconut or the almonds, half in one, half in the other. Fry, in batches, in the hot oil. Drain. Serve with dipping sauce and maybe the Daikon Radish, Mango Slaw in the salad section.

Dipping Sauce

Mix together:
½ cup coconut milk
1/3 cup peanut butter
2 tablespoons chopped fresh ginger
dash of Tabasco, if you want a little zing

TO BUTTERFLY SHRIMP

Remove legs from shrimp. Shell and tail can be removed or left on. Either way, slit shrimp down outside curve (or back), without cutting all the way through. Remove vein, (any dark colored matter in a vein down the back). Shrimp can now be flattened into a butterfly shape. Shell and tail are often left on for scampi style shrimp. They look attractive and add flavor to the sauce.

TAKA POKE

He'e is the Hawaiian word meaning squid or octopus. I once had a young friend, a Hawaiian boy with whom I worked in California, who was returning home to Hawaii. He wanted to make sure I visited him and his family the next time I was in the islands. He said to tell him a week or so before I was arriving. He would then catch some octopus and throw it up on the roof to dry before I got there, and then we'd have a feast. I somehow missed that feast but learned to love poke made from octopus. I assigned the job of finding an authentic taka poke recipe to my daughter, who recently visited Maui. She in turn, consulted her friend, Sama Mataafa. Sama consulted his "Muddah". So thanks to Laura, Sama, and Sama's Mom, we have two versions of taka poke .

Hawaiian version

1 ½ cup baby octopus or squid, chopped in bite-size pieces
1 tablespoon each, chopped green onion and white onion
1 to 2 tablespoons soy sauce
limu ogo seaweed, chopped small
chili oil or chili pepper water
Mix first 4 ingredients. Add chili seasoning to your preference of hotness. Chill 45 minutes.

Samoan version

2 cups raw ahi, aku, or uhu, chopped bite-size
2 tablespoons onion, chopped fine
½ cup cucumber, chopped small
1 tomato, chopped small
1 ½ tablespoons lemon juice
½ cup coconut milk
salt to taste
Mix and refrigerate for 45 minutes
These recipes came to me without amounts. I did it to my taste, feel free to add more of what you like best.

COQUILLES OF FISH AND SHELLFISH

You can use up all the leftover fish, shrimp, crab, squid etc. in this dish. It's so good nobody will suspect it's a leftover dinner. Actually it's so good, it's worth going out and buying fresh fish, crab etc.

¼ cup green pepper, chopped finely
½ cup celery, chopped finely
½ cup onion, chopped finely
1 cup fish, cooked
1 cup shrimp, crab, scallops or squid, any combination is fine
1 cup mayonnaise
1 tablespoon Worcestershire sauce
1 teaspoon Dijon mustard
a dash of Tabasco sauce
½ teaspoon salt
1 cup small, seasoned, croutons
½ cup parmesan cheese

Cut seafood into small bite-size pieces. Combine with onion, celery, and green pepper. Mix together the mayonnaise, mustard, Tabasco sauce, and salt. Fold into the fish mixture. Spoon into oven-proof shells (coquilles). Alternately, you can put the whole thing in a casserole dish. Top with croutons and then sprinkle on the parmesan cheese. Bake at 350 degrees for 30 minutes until hot and browned on top.

To make your own seasoned croutons, cut your favorite bread into 1 cup of cubes, ½ inch or less, for this dish. Toss cubes in 3 tablespoons olive oil, to which you have added ¼ teaspoon salt and ¼ teaspoon dried oregano. Bake on a cookie sheet at 300 degrees 5 minutes or until lightly browned.

Serves 4.

PINEAPPLE

SOY SAUCE

dried cuttlefish

ALaea sea SALT (PINK!)

things

You could expect
to find in
MAMA ANNIE'S
<u>MAUI</u> <u>kitchen</u>

(AND might want to
have on hand in
<u>YOUR OWN</u> !)

dried STAR ANISE

PRAWN

dried WASABI (hot!)

CILANTRO

tofu

CURRY POWDER

white PEPPER

POI

RICE NOODLES

PAPAYA

GUAVA

PANKO JAPANESE BREADCRUMBS

MAHi MAHi STEAK

OPAH FILLet (MOONFish!)

MISO

CANNED HAWAIIAN COCONUT MILK

SALMON (good FOR LOMi LOMi)

TARO LEAF (FOR LAU LAU)

butter (haole secret ingredient)

SOBA NOODLES

good wooden SPOON
(FOR stirring + chasing kids out of kitchen)

fish sauce

tuna
(good for poke)

MAUI
ONION

SeSame
oiL

KALUA
Pig

MACADAMIA
Nuts

szechuan
chili paste
(hot!!!)

PASSION
fruit

dRied
shiitake
mushrooms

OPAKA PAKA
filLet

fresh
ginger

NORi
dRied
SeaweeD

JAPANESe OR
CALRoSe RiCe

coconut

☆ MAMA ANNie ☆
(helpful to
have on hand)

SPAM
SPAM

goba
(seSAme seeds)

gLass of wine
(good for spirits
whiLe
cooking!)

Ripe
tomato
(MAiNLAND
import)

fermented
bLack
beans

AppLe bANANAs

LeMONgRASS

MANgo

CHinese
hoisin
sauce

hawAiiAN
Potato
chips
(mmmm!)

ONAGA
fillet

Rice wine
vinegar

GARLiC

ONO (ANother
"O" fish)

PORTUGUESE SQUID

In the late 1800's boatload after boatload of Portuguese laborers came to the islands to work in the plantation fields. They can be thanked for bringing the ukelele to Hawaii. The Hawaiians, who love music, were delighted with it and named it "jumping flea", ukelele in Hawaiian. They also brought their culture and their food adding a spicy Mediterranean flavor to the local cuisine. The following is a typical Portuguese dish that traveled well to Hawaii. It's a simple dish using fresh tomatoes and onions which grow very well in the islands. Use as good an olive oil as you can find and buy the smallest squid you can find.

2 pounds small squid
2 onions
¼ cup chopped parsley
salt and pepper
2 cups chopped, fresh, tomatoes
¼ cup extra-virgin olive oil

Buy your squid already cleaned, or ask the butcher to clean it for you. Cut into bite sized pieces. Slice the onions thin. Heat the olive oil and sauté the onions for 2 or 3 minutes over medium heat. Add the parsley and cook until vegetables are soft but not brown. Sprinkle lightly with pepper. Add squid and cover with tomatoes. Cover and simmer for just a few minutes until squid is cooked and tomatoes are heated. Add salt to taste. This is good with hot French bread.

COCONUT SHRIMP

2 pounds jumbo shrimp
1 cup flour
½ teaspoon salt
½ teaspoon sugar
1 egg, slightly beaten
2 tablespoons oil
1 cup ice water
¾ cup grated coconut
¼ cup minced macadamia nuts*
oil for frying

Mix flour, salt, sugar, egg, oil, and water. Beat lightly until smooth. Allow to sit while you clean and devein shrimp. Leave tails on shrimp, they make good handles. Combine coconut with the macadamia nuts. Heat frying oil. Dip shrimp into batter, then into coconut mix. Fry in oil until light brown. Drain on paper towels.

Mincing macadamia nuts has to be done by hand. Since they contain a lot of oil, most food processors make a paste of them rather quickly.

ALASKAN HALIBUT WITH PAPAYA SALSA

This could be made with any firm white fish, ono or sea bass come to mind. It's nice served with snow peas or roasted zucchini.

1½ to 2 pounds fish, cut in 4 pieces
6 tablespoons soy sauce
2 tablespoons seasoned rice vinegar
1 tablespoon vegetable oil
2 teaspoons sugar
Papaya Salsa

Make the salsa and refrigerate.
Combine soy sauce, vinegar, oil and sugar. Brush fish lightly on both sides with this mixture and transfer the rest to a small saucepan. Grill or boil fish 3 to 4 minutes per side, depending on thickness, until center flakes easily. Heat reserved soy sauce mixture and divide between 4 plates. Top with 1 piece of fish. Top fish with a scoop of the Papaya Salsa.

Serves 4

PAPAYA SALSA

1 Papaya, peeled and cut ¼ inch
¼ cup shallot or onion, chopped small
1 tablespoon red bell pepper, minced
½ jalapeno pepper, minced
1 tablespoon fresh ginger, minced
2 tablespoons seasoned rice vinegar
2 teaspoons sugar
salt to taste

Combine all ingredients. If you want it hotter add the other half of the jalapeno, minced, or a couple of dashes hot sauce.

58

Meat and Poultry

MARINATED FLANK STEAK FOR BBQ

This is sooo good! Start the marinade a day or two before the picnic, then just slap them on the grill for a few minutes on each side. The vegetables tenderize the meat. Great with 1 scoop macaroni salad, 2 scoop rice. Also great in a tortilla with salsa and shredded lettuce. Cut in small strips for tortilla version.

2 pounds flank steak
½ cup water
½ cup soy sauce
1 small onion, coarsely chopped
2 large cloves garlic, minced
1 tablespoon minced fresh ginger
¼ cup brown sugar
1 tablespoon hot mustard or 1 teaspoon mustard powder
1 tablespoon sesame oil
2 tablespoons sesame seed

Cut flank steak on an extreme angle into strips 2 inches wide. Mix together remaining ingredients in a ceramic or stainless steel dish large enough to hold the steak. Add steak and turn to coat the meat with the marinade. Cover and leave in refrigerator for 1 to 3 days, turning occasionally. Cook to your liking on a hot grill.

SWEET AND SOUR SPARE RIBS

Spice rub (recipe below)
2 pounds spare ribs

Sauce

½ cup honey
½ cup vinegar
1 tablespoon minced fresh ginger
¼ cup soy sauce
½ cup catsup
1 small can crushed pineapple

Cut spareribs into serving racks, 3 or 4 per serving. Rub well with spice rub. Combine the rest of the ingredients in a saucepan and simmer on low, for 10 minutes. Cook ribs, covered, on grill, for 30 to 45 minutes, depending on thickness. Brush with sauce the last 5 minutes and serve with the extra sauce on the side for dunking.

Spice Rub

1 tablespoon salt
1 tablespoon sugar
½ teaspoon pepper
½ teaspoon cayenne pepper
1 teaspoon paprika
1 teaspoon onion powder

Combine well.

Serves about 4 people.

PUEO, THE OWL GOD

In the beautiful Manoa Valley, nestled against some of the highest peaks in Oahu, an endless maelstrom of soft breezes, warm rains, and brilliant sun, creates a wonderland of shimmering color, as one rainbow vies with another until they are piled in arches over the cliffs and valleys. Since ancient times, this has been the home of the royal chiefs and of the rainbow maiden, Ka-hala. It is also the home of the owl god of this girl's family.

Ka-hala had been promised to a chief of Waikiki, who unbeknownst to her parents, was a foul fellow with a nasty temper. The chief came after her and led her on a long journey to the lower end of the valley. When the maiden became weary and could walk no more, the cad beat her with a bunch of hala nuts and killed her, burying her body under a pile of leaves and dirt. Pueo, the owl god was watching over her and as soon as the chief left, he dug up her body and carried her back to the head of the valley, where he restored her life.

Twice more, the vile chief came for her and dragged her over ridges, raging streams, deep valleys and up the next ridge. When she tired, he again beat her to death and buried her. Pueo, each time, rescued her and blew life back into her.

Many waterfalls plunge over the precipitous cliffs at the head of Manoa valley, The longest and widest of these are said to be made of the tears of Ka-hala as she suffered at the hands of the cruel chief.

BRAISED PORK

This is pork for all occasions. It is very good as is. It's a good picnic dish as it jumps right into a sandwich or a tortilla. You can add it to a salad, soup or chow fun. I always make a large amount and freeze the leftovers in small portions to add where I need it. Char sui is an Asian version of roast pork that is very popular in Hawaii. I've included a recipe for that as well.

3 pound pork butt or shoulder roast
2 teaspoons coarse rock or sea salt
1 tablespoon sugar
1 teaspoon black pepper
½ teaspoon cayenne pepper
2 tablespoons oil
Bar B Q sauce*

Mix dry ingredients and rub well into meat. Heat oil in skillet and brown meat well on all sides. Remove meat to ovenproof roasting pan and add 2 cups Bar B Q sauce. Cover tightly and cook 2 to 3 hours at 350 degrees. Serve with extra BAR B Q sauce on the side.

* Any favorite Bar B Q sauce will do. There's a good one on the facing page.

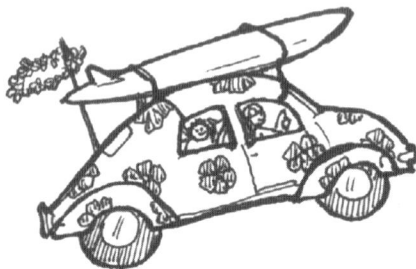

CHAR SUI MARINADE

3 pound pork butt or tenderloin
2 teaspoons sea salt
1 tablespoon sugar
½ cup soy sauce
½ cup hoisin sauce
½ cup rice wine or sherry
1 tablespoon grated fresh ginger
½ teaspoon Chinese 5-spice

Cut pork in 2 inch wide strips, the length of the roast. Marinate 6 to 8 hours or over night. Roast for 1 ½ to 2 hours, covered until last 20 minutes, or grill until done and edges are crispy.

PLUM BAR B Q SAUCE

1 cup catsup
½ cup coffee
½ cup vinegar
3 tablespoons Worcestershire sauce
3 tablespoons Dijon mustard, or any spicy mustard
4 tablespoons plum jam
salt to taste

Mix all ingredients except salt in a saucepan and simmer for 5 minutes. Cool and add salt if needed.

PORTUGUESE POT ROAST

3 to 4 pound pot roast, rump or 7 bone

Rub

1 teaspoon salt
½ teaspoon pepper
1 teaspoon paprika
1 teaspoon sugar

¼ cup flour
2 tablespoons oil
1 cup red wine
1 cup beef bouillon
2 tablespoons vinegar
1 tablespoon horseradish
2 bay leaves
1 large onion, chopped
2 cloves garlic, minced
1 tablespoon dark brown sugar

Mix salt, pepper, paprika and sugar together and rub well into meat. Dredge meat with flour. Heat oil in ovenproof skillet or Dutch oven and brown meat on all sides. Mix the rest of the ingredients and pour over meat. Cover tightly and cook on low for 3 to 4 hours. Make sure liquid doesn't boil, as boiling toughens meat. Vegetables such as potatoes, carrots, or mushrooms may be added for the last half hour of cooking.

When, after years of yearning, I finally got to Moloka'i, I rented a car from one of the most charming women I've ever met. I can't recommend her business highly enough. It's called Molokai Island Kine Auto Rental, accessible on the internet. You will not only get a fine car, you will get met and greeted at the airport and then you get to deal with Barbara. You will get tips on where to go on the island including where and at what hour to go get Hawaiian sweet bread hot out of the oven. She will tell you not to drive too fast because the police aren't always happy to be stationed on Moloka'i. She knows where to get island kine food and where to take your picnics.

 A year after I rented a car from her, I e- mailed her and asked if she had any favorite family recipes she wouldn't mind sharing with me. I got an immediate response with the two following recipes. She said " Here are two recipes that I use either for large groups or for our own family (never less than 10).

MIRIN CHIX WINGS

3 to 5 pounds chicken wings
2/3 cup soy sauce
1/3 cup mirin (Japanese rice wine)
1/3 cup sugar
1 teaspoon grated fresh ginger
1 teaspoon sesame oil
flour for dredging
salt
oil for frying

Rinse chicken wings and pat dry with paper towels. Sprinkle lightly with salt and dredge in flour. Combine remaining ingredients and bring to a boil in a saucepan. Turn down and simmer just until sugar dissolves. Heat oil and fry chicken wings until cooked through and crispy, about 8 to 10 minutes. Drain on paper towels. Serve with sauce for dipping.

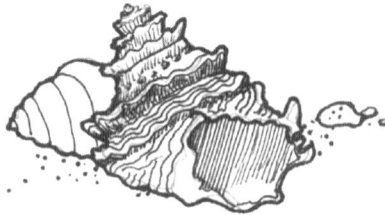

CURRIED CHICKEN

Barbara specified chicken wings in this recipe which I like very much, but I think thighs would work well too.

5 pounds chicken wings, and/or thighs
½ cup (or more) vegetable oil
1 large onion
3 to 4 garlic cloves, minced
2 to 3 teaspoons curry powder
1 large or 2 small cans chicken broth
2 large potatoes, cut into ½ inch cubes
2 carrots, sliced ¼ inch
1 cup corn kernels, canned or fresh
1 cup peas*
6 ounces coconut milk
flour or cornstarch for thickening
hot rice

Heat oil in skillet and brown chicken pieces in batches, adding more oil if necessary. Remove chicken and adding more oil if necessary, sauté onion and garlic a few minutes. Add curry powder, mix in and sauté a minute more. Add chicken broth and vegetables. Bring to a boil, turn down to a simmer and cook until chicken is done and vegetables are tender, 15 to 20 minutes. Add coconut milk. If sauce is too thin, mix 2 tablespoonfuls corn starch or flour to 2 tablespoonfuls water. Mix and add a little at a time and simmer until desired thickness. Serve over hot rice.

* These vegetables can be substituted to suit your taste. If you don't like peas, try zucchini, or mushrooms, and so on.

CRISPY PINEAPPLE CHICKEN

My family gives this recipe a great rating.(Do you believe the ingrates rate my recipes?) It's a wonderful contrast of sweet and tangy and crispy and soft. One of the kids said it tasted like pineapple upside down cake with chicken in it.

Oil for stir-fry
1 onion
1 large clove garlic, chopped
1 tablespoon chopped, fresh, ginger
½ jalapeno pepper, chopped
1 cup pineapple chunks
½ cup pineapple juice
1 cup chicken broth
2 tablespoons dark brown sugar
2 tablespoons rice vinegar
½ teaspoon sea salt
2 chicken breasts, skinned and boned
½ cup rice powder or flour
½ teaspoon sea salt
½ package thin noodles, angel hair or Asian noodles
2 handfuls bean sprouts

Cut the onion in half from top to bottom, then cut into wedge shaped slices from top to bottom. Heat 2 tablespoons oil in large skillet and stir-fry onions 2 or 3 minutes. Add garlic, ginger and jalapeno and stir-fry a few minutes more. Add pineapple juice, chicken, broth, pineapple, brown sugar, rice vinegar and ½ teaspoon salt. Cook over medium heat 8 to 10 minutes or until liquid is reduced and a little syrupy. Slice chicken breasts into bite size pieces. Mix rice flour with water to a consistency of thick soup and add ½ teaspoon salt. Heat 4 tablespoons oil in smaller skillet. Put chicken pieces into rice flour batter and coat well. Cook in hot oil, in batches so as not to crowd until quite crispy and browned. Remove to paper towels to drain. Cook noodles in boiling, salted water, adding bean sprouts for last 2 minutes. Drain and divide onto 4 serving plates. Add chicken to pineapple sauce and serve over noodles.Serves 3 or 4.

RAMEN WITH TURKEY

Everybody loves ramen! I invented this recipe in order to make a meal out of it. It's fast, easy and delicious. You could use chicken or pork just as well as turkey.

Oil for stir-fry
1 package Ramen noodles
½ cup turkey breast pieces, cooked or raw
2 small sausages, cooked and sliced
¾ cup shredded cabbage
2 green onions
1 carrot
1 small cucumber
1 teaspoon minced fresh ginger
4 tablespoons rice vinegar
¼ cup oyster sauce*

Peel and seed cucumber. Cut cucumber, carrot and green onions into julienne slices.
 Prepare ramen according to directions on package. Heat 2 tablespoons oil, add onion and turkey if turkey is raw. Cook until onion starts to get tender and turkey is white, 2 or 3 minutes. Add more oil if needed. Add cabbage and carrots, cook 3 minutes more. Add sausage, turkey if it was precooked, cucumber and ginger. Cook 1 minute. Add vinegar and oyster sauce and cook just until combined and heated through. Divide ramen into four bowls and top with turkey mixture.

Oyster sauce is available in the Asian section of most supermarkets

Serves 4.

PORK ROAST WITH FRUIT

3 to 4 pound pork loin
1 teaspoon dried or powdered sage
salt and pepper
1 cup chicken broth or water
3 tablespoons guava jelly
grated rind and juice of 1 orange
1 cup Mirin or sherry
fruit, guava, oranges, lychees*
1 teaspoon corn starch
more broth or water if necessary

Mix salt, pepper, and sage and rub into pork. Place in a roasting pan with ½ the water or broth. Cook, uncovered for 2 hours at 325 degrees. Half way through the roasting remove pan from oven. Pour off as much of the fat as you can, reserving as much of the pan juices as you can. Cover top of roast with jelly and then orange rind. Pour Mirin or sherry and orange juice over meat, and continue roasting until done (170 degrees on the meat thermometer). Remove meat to a platter. Add remaining half cup broth or water to pan and scrape up drippings. Thicken gravy with 1 teaspoon corn starch mixed with 1/3 cup water. Add more broth or water to make gravy proper thickness. Season with salt and pepper. Add fruit to gravy and heat for 1 minute. Serve fruit on platter around meat and pour gravy over the top or serve it separately. I like this with steamed rice or polenta.

JAMBALAYA, HAWAIIAN STYLE

Hawaii has all the ingredients to make a home-version jambalaya that will rival the New Orleans one.

2 tablespoons canola oil, or any vegetable oil
2 fat cloves garlic, minced
2 cups Maui onions, chopped
1 green pepper and one red pepper, cut in thin slices
6 chicken thighs
½ to ¾ pounds Portuguese sausage, cut in chunks
1 pound shellfish, shrimp, scallops or lobster
2 bay leaves
3 or 4 large Maui tomatoes, peeled and chopped*
5 cups chicken broth
2 cups rice
salt
cayenne pepper or hot sauce (like Tabasco)

Heat the oil in a Dutch oven or large skillet. Wash and dry chicken thighs and brown on each side in heated oil. Add the onion and peppers and sauté over medium heat for 5 minutes. Add the garlic for the last minute. Garlic gets bitter if it browns. Add the sausage, the bay leaves, the tomatoes and the salt. Add a few shakes hot sauce OR ¼ teaspoon cayenne. Stir, cook 1 minute and taste. If you want it hotter, add more. The rice and chicken broth will absorb some of the heat. Add the chicken broth and stir in the rice. Cover and cook on low heat for 15 minutes. Add the shellfish. Cover again and cook 5 or 6 minutes more, or until the rice is done.

Tomatoes can be easily peeled by immersing them in very hot water for 1 minute.

Serves 6

ADOBO

Between 1907 and 1941, 125,000 Filipinos were brought to Hawaii as contract laborers. They were valued as people with a sunny disposition who were easy to work with. Thousands stayed and they and their subsequent families adapted well to life on the islands, while keeping many of their own traditions. Adobo is a national dish in the Philippines and now can be found in many kitchens in Hawaii.

1 chicken, cut in serving pieces
1 pound pork, not too lean, cut in strips
5 cloves garlic
½ cup cider vinegar
2 cups water
1 teaspoon salt
scant teaspoon peppercorns
1 bay leaf

Smash garlic cloves. Bruise* the peppercorns in a mortar and pestle. Combine both with vinegar, water, salt, and bay leaf. Add meat and marinate for an hour. Transfer to heavy pot, cover and simmer on low for 2 to 3 hours, until liquid is absorbed and meat is tender. Serve with steamed white rice.

* Bruise means just breaking them enough to release the flavor. Smash sounds a little brutal on the garlic cloves too, actually you want to squish them, to expose the flavorful inside.

STUFFED CHICKEN BREAST

This is such a great dish. You can use up a bunch of leftovers and it looks and tastes like you just graduated from a culinary institute. My alpha male enthusiastic eater said, "Where did you get this recipe?" I said, " Oh you know, I was just cleaning out the refrigerator." He said, "PLEASE write this one down."

4 chicken breasts, skinned and boned
½ cup flour
oil for frying
½ cup ham, spam, sausage, or salami, diced small
1 cup cooked greens, chard, spinach, or collard greens
2 green onions, chopped small
½ cup crumbled feta, or grated white cheese, Jack, Fontina, etc.
1 cup+ chicken broth
½ cup sliced dried mango, or apricot

Sprinkle flour on chopping board and place chicken breasts on flour. Pound to flatten until they are 1/3 inch thick or so. Turn often to keep them floured. Divide greens among the 4 breasts spreading them up to ½ inch from the edges. Spread onions, meat, and cheese over the greens. Roll chicken breasts and secure with a toothpick or tie with kitchen string. Cover bottom of a deep skillet or Dutch oven with a thin layer of oil. Heat and add chicken rolls. Brown well on all sides. Add chicken broth and mango slices and cook 20 minutes more on low heat. Remove breasts from pan and slice ½ inch thick. Alternately, serve them whole. Cover with sauce left in pan.

Note: I made this dish with mango which I purchased in an Asian market. I doubt if it's hard to find, most health food stores probably have it. If you can't find it or can't be bothered I think dried apricots will be just as good and they're everywhere.

ONE GOOD MEAT LOAF

Make two, they're gonna' love this one. I serve it with beans and sauteed cabbage

1 pound hamburger
½ pound mild pork sausage
1 onion, chopped
2 tablespoons olive oil
1 teaspoon ground cumin
1 tablespoon toasted Mexican oregano
½ teaspoon chipotle powder
½ teaspoon salt and a few shakes of pepper.
½ pound smoked cheddar cheese, cut in cubes.
¼ cup worsteshire sauce

Mix the hamburger and sausage together in a large bowl. Saute the onions with the cumin in the olive oil until starting to get tender and brown. Add to the meat. Add the oregano to the frying pan and toast for 2 to 3 minutes. Add to the meat mixture. Add the chipotle and the salt and pepper. Fold in the cheese cubes. Put mixture into loof pan and bake in a 350 degree oven for 1 hour.

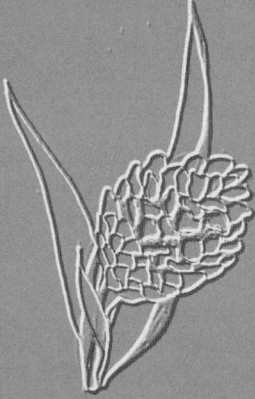

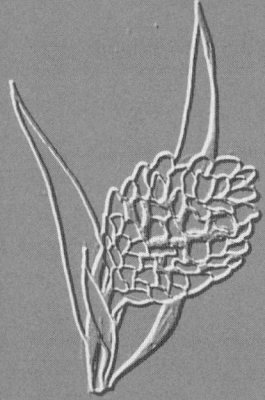

Luaus and Hukilaus

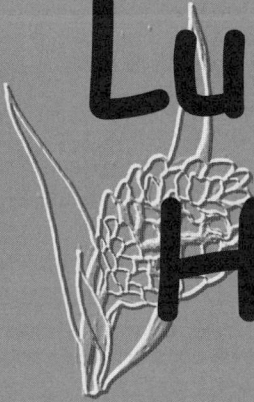

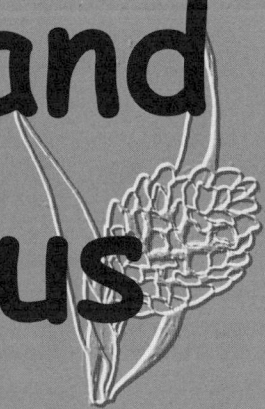

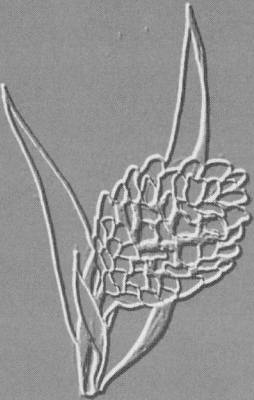

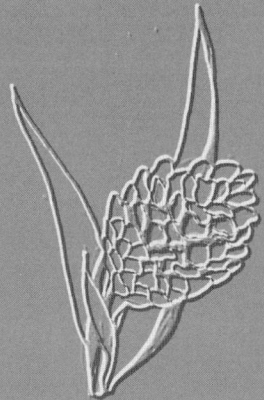

SHUT 'EM UP CHILI

So named because it keeps 'em all quiet while they're waiting for the pig to get cooked. In Hawaii, chili is often served over white rice. I like the combo very much.

1½ to 2 pounds pork, cut in cubes
1 large onion, coarsely chopped
2 large cloves garlic, chopped
1 large can diced tomatoes
1 4 ounce can tomato paste
2 tablespoons red wine or cider vinegar
2 to 3 cups water
1 small can chopped jalapenos
3 cans beans, any combination of pinto, black or kidney
1 heaping tablespoon of each of the following spices:
mild chili powder
cumin
oregano
paprika
sugar
1 teaspoon salt, ½ teaspoon pepper
Add, ½ teaspoon at a time, hot chili powder
(you need to test for hotness as you add this)
3 to 4 cups cooked white rice

Over medium heat, brown pork, onions and garlic in a sturdy pan, lightly oiled, 5 minutes or so. Add everything else, turn the heat down and cook for at least an hour and a half. You can leave it on very low heat all day if you want.

LAULAU

Laulau is a very popular dish in Hawaii. It seems to me to be one of the purely Polynesian dishes. All the ingredients are indigenous and one can easily imagine ancient people wrapping their pork and fish in leaves and placing them in the imu pit with sweet potatoes and bananas. There are lots of variations. Chicken replaces pork and all kinds of fish are used. Spinach leaves can be substituted for the taro. Banana leaves or even corn husks can be used instead of the traditional ti leaves. I have sometimes added mango or pineapple slices. A slice of Maui onion sounds good in there as well. Here is the traditional recipe. Do with it what you will.

Taro or spinach leaves
1 pound pork, shoulder or butt
¾ pounds white fish, ono or opah are good
1 tablespoon 'alaea salt* or rock salt
Ti leaves

Cut pork and fish, each in 8 pieces. Rub pork with salt. Wash all leaves. Overlap 3 to 5 taro leaves to form a wrap and place 1 piece of pork on it. Put a piece of fish on top of the pork. Make a package by folding leaves around pork and fish. Make 7 more packages. Remove stem and stiff ribs from ti leaves. Place laulau package on ti leaf. Wrap and tie with string. Put in a steamer over simmering water and cook 4 to 6 hours, adding water if necessary.

See table of contents for 'alaea salt.

KIM CHEE

There are as many versions of kim chee as there are of stew. Chinese cabbage, bok choy, or Napa cabbage, and salt seem to be the common denominator. It's a delightful and sophisticated salad and provides a tangy crunch to to a bland meal. The Koreans make it quite hot but you can adjust that to your taste.

1 head Chinese Napa cabbage or bok choy, sliced thin
1 daikon radish, thinly sliced
1 cucumber, thinly sliced
2 large cloves garlic, minced
¼ cup sea salt
1 tablespoon sea salt
¾ cup water
½ cup white vinegar
1 tablespoon, or more, fresh ginger, minced
1 tablespoon minced garlic
1 tablespoon, or more, dried chili flakes

Layer cabbage, radish, and cucumber in large bowl or crock. Sprinkle the 1/4 cup salt between the layers. Cover with water and vinegar. Place a bowl or plate on top, to keep vegetables submerged, and leave overnight. Place vegetables in a colander and rinse very well. Return to crock and add garlic, ginger, 1 tablespoon salt (or less) and chili flakes. Toss well. Add water. Cover tightly and refrigerate for 3 days. Stir every day. Kim chee is served as a side dish with meat or sometimes alone with rice.

MEATBALL HERO SANDWHICHES

This is a good party dish. It can be made several days ahead if you wish. It can easily be doubled. People can serve themselves and kids of all ages like it.

1 pound ground beef
½ pound ground pork
1 small onion, chopped small
2 cloves garlic, minced
¾ cup dried breadcrumbs
1 egg
¼ cup catsup
2 tablespoons Worcestershire sauce
1 teaspoon dried basil
1 teaspoon dried marjoram
½ teaspoon salt
¼ tsp freshly ground pepper
2 tablespoons oil
4 cups tomato sauce
2 loaves French bread

Combine all but the last 3 ingredients in a large bowl. Form into balls 1 inch or so in diameter. Heat oil in frying pan and brown meatballs in batches. Add the tomato sauce, cover and simmer, on low, for 25 minutes. Slice bread loaves in half longwise and fill with meatballs and sauce. Shredded lettuce or cabbage, cheese or sliced onions may be added on top. Cut into individual servings.

Serves 2 really big guys or 10

MENEHUNE

When visiting the Hawaiian Islands, it is prudent to keep an eye out for Menehunes. Most places in the world have a sub-culture of 'little people'. Leprechauns, fairies, trolls, pixies and Menehunes are examples of these. The Menehunes of Hawaii are a small, squat tribe of people. They are described as 2 to 3 feet tall, dark and rather hairy, and very strong. Their voices are deep and gruff and their laughter loud and ringing. There is a sub sub- culture of the Menehunes, called the Mu, or banana eating people.

The cave-dwelling Menehune worked only at night, accomplishing great feats, such as building heiau or roads and very often, walled fishponds. The heiau or temple structures attributed to the Menehune are said to be the oldest heiau in each of the islands. There is one on a cliff in Molokai at Waikolu valley that no one has been able to reach from the top or the bottom. Unreachable trails and caves can still be seen on the formidable cliffs of Kauai.

 All work had to be finished in one night, but finished or not, work stopped at the first sign of light. There are still unfinished walls all over the islands, mute testimony to the poor job estimate of a Menehune. Most jobs, however, were finished in time for play. Play included jumping from cliffs into the sea, top spinning, shooting arrows, foot races and hand wrestling.
Within the many versions of the myths, there are descriptions of complicated social structures, including chiefs and their kahunas (wisemen), astrologers, story-tellers, minstrels and musicians. Rich stories of love, pure and illicit, children stolen and ransomed, heroic journeys and migrations, abound. The people are brave and wild, mischievous or evil, beautiful and grotesque. The Menehunes were said to be kind and very helpful to those who were good to them and and to those who weren't, and even those among their own who pushed the boundaries of acceptable behavior, the punishment was swift and final. People were often turned to stone.

The little stone or carved wood Tiki Gods that you buy in souvenir shops are said to resemble Menehunes. It would be impossible to separate the historical basis of these legends from the imaginative interpretation that has gone on for hundreds of years. The genealogists are working on it, but for most of us, they are just highly entertaining reading.

MANAPUA

Manapua is a steamed bun with a filling in the middle. It is the same thing as the Bao you get at a Dim Sum restaurant. The filling can be meat or sweet bean paste or any number of other things but the most common and, I think the best, is char sui, which is seasoned pork. The dough is a typical yeast dough, not difficult to make. Some people prefer to use the frozen white bread dough that you can find in any grocery story freezer. Use it the same as you use the completed dough in the recipe below.

1 package or 1 tablespoon active dry yeast
1 cup warm water
3 ¼ to 3 ½ cups flour
¼ cup sugar
1 rounded tablespoon vegetable oil
filling (there is a recipe for char sui on the facing page)

Dissolve yeast in water. Add sugar and oil. Stir to combine and dissolve sugar. Mix in flour until you have a stiff dough. Dust a chopping board with flour and knead dough until smooth and elastic. Place dough in a greased bowl, cover, and allow to rise in a warm place for 2 to 4 hours. Divide into 18 or 20 pieces. Shape into flat rounds . Place filling in center. Bring up sides and pinch together at the top. Place each on a square of paper and let rest for ½ hour. Steam for 15 minutes.

CHAR SUI FILLING

½ pound roasted or braised pork
2 cloves garlic, minced
¼ cup chopped green onions
2 tablespoons minced water chestnuts(optional)
½ cup Bar B Q sauce
2 tablespoons orange marmalade or plum jelly
few shakes chili oil
1 tablespoon cooking oil

Dice pork no larger than ½ inch pieces. Heat cooking oil in fry pan. Sauté onions and pork until onions are soft. Add garlic and water chestnuts and cook 2 minutes longer. Mix in Bar B Q sauce, marmalade or jelly, and chili oil. Cook just until combined and thickened.

CHOW FUN

I love Chow Fun. I first tasted it as I was leaving the Maui County Fair to catch a flight to the mainland. I asked a few people on my way out how to make it and was answered by grins and shrugs. On arriving, late, at the airport, I found I was the only one in line to get my boarding pass so I asked the girl behind the counter. She said, "Oh sure, fry up a little meat with a few vegetables and stir your noodles in. I have elaborated slightly on this. Chow Fun noodles are traditionally wide and flat, much like fettucine. 'Fun' in the name means the noodles are usually made of rice flour but this dish can stand lots of substitutions.

3 tablespoons oil, for stir frying
½ cup diced meat; pork, chicken or shrimp, cooked
¼ cup green onion, chopped small
2 tablespoons carrots, chopped small
2 tablespoons mushrooms, chopped small
1 tablespoon parsley, chopped small
Chow Fun noodles*
salt to taste

Heat oil, add onion and carrot and stir fry 2 or 3 minutes until vegetables start to soften. Stir in mushrooms and meat and cook 2 more minutes. Add parsley and cook 1 more minute. Gently stir in noodles and heat through. Salt to taste.

* If you can't find Chow Fun noodles, you can use fettucine or egg noodles. Cook them until just tender.

CONE SUSHI

I see very little cone sushi outside of Hawaii. Occasionally a sushi platter will have a couple of them but I suspect they aren't as popular on the mainland as they are in the islands. They may also be rampant in Japan, I don't know, I haven't been there. I think they are a perfect snack. They look like little footballs and can be eaten easily with the fingers. Basically, they are made up of a wad of rice in a tofu wrapper. I often lace the rice with whatever's on hand , but I like them plain as well. The tofu wraps are called aburaage. The brand I buy is Hinoichi and the package says, "Age, French fried tofu pouches".

1 package tofu pouches
1 cup short grain rice
1 teaspoon sugar
2 tablespoons sugar
4 tablespoons rice vinegar
1 teaspoon salt

Put rice in heavy pan. Add 1 teaspoon sugar to 1 ¼ cup cold water . Add to rice and soak 2 hours. Cover and bring to quick boil. Turn heat to low and cook 10 minutes. Remove from heat and allow to sit 10 minutes. Do not remove lid during this process. Mix 2 tablespoons sugar with rice vinegar and salt in a small saucepan and heat to dissolve sugar. Turn rice into a cold bowl, mix in vinegar mixture and turn out on a board to cool. Spread rice to hasten cooling. This prevents sogginess. When rice is cool, add whatever you'd like and stuff into aburaage, taking care not to tear pouches.

Ideas for 'lacing the rice'. Add small pieces of: Spam, ham, pork, flaked fish, scrambled egg, mushrooms, pickled plum, chives, leftover cooked vegetables or litchi nuts.

POKE

Poke is enormously popular in Hawaii. As they have chili cook-offs in the southwestern United States, they have Poke cook-offs in Hawaii, even though it is seldom cooked. This means, of course, that once you get the hang of it, you can do whatever you like with it. You need very fresh Ahi, as it is usually used raw, but not always. In fact, Ahi is just the traditional main ingredient. I have seen other fish used and even tofu instead of fish. The following recipe should be considered a jumping off point for you. Good luck.

1 Pound Ahi, sashimi grade
½ Maui or Vidalia onion, chopped small
1 large clove garlic, minced
1 small cucumber, peeled, seeded and chopped ¼ inch
1 teaspoon minced lemon grass or fresh ginger
2 teaspoons toasted sesame seeds
1 tablespoon soy sauce
1 tablespoon vegetable oil
½ teaspoon sesame oil
few drops chili oil

Cut Ahi into bite sized pieces. Combine with onion, garlic, cucumber, lemon grass or ginger, and sesame seeds. Combine the soy sauce and the three oils and mix into fish mixture. Chill.

Serves 6 to 8

MAC NUT MUNCHIES

My friend, Sandy has been making these for 20 years. She says they're always a hit.

1 7-9 ounce package macadamia nuts
2 tablespoons melted butter
½ teaspoon seasoned salt (use your favorite)
¼ teaspoon hot pepper sauce
¼ teaspoon paprika
¼ teaspoon garlic salt or powder

Combine all ingredients in a baking pan. Bake 10 minutes at 375 degrees, stirring once or twice during baking. Drain on paper towels and serve hot or at room temperature.

PINEAPPLE POPCORN

And one for the kids of all ages.

5 cups lightly salted popcorn
½ to 1 cup nuts, cut in large pieces
2/3 cups sugar
¼ cup water
¼ cup frozen pineapple concentrate
2 ½ tablespoons white corn syrup
1/8 teaspoon salt
½ teaspoon white vinegar

Boil sugar, water, frozen pineapple, and corn syrup, stirring until sugar is dissolved. Cook to a firm ball, 248 degrees on a candy thermometer. Add the 1/8 teaspoon salt and vinegar, bring to hard ball stage, 290 degrees. Pour hot syrup slowly over popcorn and nuts and mix in well. Spread mixture on a baking sheet and cool. Break into pieces.

MIZUTAKI

This, as you may guess from the name, is a Japanese recipe. It is one of my favorite party recipes. Mizutaki means 'boiling water'. Basically you need a pot of boiling water (I use broth) and meats and vegetables of your choice to cook in it. Traditionally, the pot is in the middle of the table on a hot plate, or you can use an electric skillet or pan. I find you need a pot for every 4 people. The water or broth is brought to a boil, then pieces of beef, chicken or fish, and various vegetables are placed in the pot until cooked, then removed to individual plates and replaced by the next item. The pieces of food are dipped into sauces that are served on the side. Then, as my darling sister-in-law, Kayoko, puts it, "the fun isn't over yet". The now very flavorful broth , is served, with or without noodles or sometimes eggs, to end the meal.
for each pot:

1 49.5 ounce can chicken broth
2 chicken breasts, cut in bite size pieces
½ pound raw top sirloin or filet, sliced thin
8 or 12 shrimp
12 mushrooms, fresh shitake are good
1 bunch spinach, napa cabbage or other greens
1 bunch green onions, cut in 2 inch pieces
1 medium yam, cut in ¼ inch slices
1 small package rice noodles or 4 eggs.

You can cook these in any order you want. I usually start with a chicken 'course', then alternate between the vegetables and meats or fish. When all the food is eaten, add the noodles to the broth and cook 5 minutes or so, until done and serve the broth and noodles in bowls. Alternately, you can add 4 eggs and poach for 3 to 4 minutes or until done to your liking. Recipes for sauces are on the following page.
These ingredients are further suggestions: firm fish cut in chunks, thin slices of pork, summer squashes or any vegetable that cooks fairly quickly.
Serves 4.

SAUCES FOR MIZUTAKI

Sesame Sauce

6 tablespoons white sesame seeds
½ teaspoon salt
2 tablespoons white vinegar
4 tablespoons water
1 tablespoon soy sauce
2 tablespoons mirin (rice wine) or dry sherry

Put sesame seeds with water in a blender and puree. Add other ingredients and mix just until blended. Adjust seasoning. This should be fairly salty as your broth or water is without added salt. Salt it to your taste.

Creamy Mizutaki Sauce

This is basically a homemade mayonnaise sauce. They have come up with a salmonella proof egg that is a little more expensive, but well worth it in my opinion, since I love homemade sauces. 2 eggs, 2 tablespoons vinegar, 2 cups salad oil, ½ cup sour cream, 4 tablespoons soy sauce, 4 tablespoons mirin or sherry. Blend eggs with vinegar. While blending, add oil slowly in a steady stream. Stir in remaining ingredients.

Chili Sauce

It is not at all traditional to serve a hot sauce with Japanese food but I love them so I usually serve one of each at each plate, one traditional sauce and one hot sauce.

2 small red fresh chilies
2 shallots, and 2 garlic cloves chopped small
1 tablespoon grated fresh ginger
2 tablespoons sugar
¼ teaspoon salt
3 tablespoons white vinegar

Very carefully, seed and coarsely chop the chilis. Wear rubber gloves or wash hands thoroughly after handling. Blend all ingredients until smooth.

RAW FISH IN COCONUT MILK

The fish in Hawaii is always so fresh that many recipes call for it raw. Sashimi is thinly sliced raw fish, often ahi, usually served with soy sauce and wasabi (green horseradish paste). Poke is raw fish combined with anything the chef comes up with and they do come up with a lot of variations. I think fish, especially white fish, blends very well with coconut, so I'm very fond of this recipe.

1 pound white fish, ono, opah, mahi-mahi
½ cup freshly squeezed lime juice, about 4 limes
2 green onions, chopped small
½ teaspoon salt
1 cup coconut milk

Cut fish into small bite sized pieces and place in a bowl. Cover with the lime juice and refrigerate for 4 to 6 hours. Drain off the liquid. Add onions and salt to fish. Mix and add the coconut milk.

Serves 8 as an appetizer

IMU PIGS AND POI

IMU PIG

Well, I've got to admit it, I've never cooked a pig in an Imu oven. I've eaten both pork and beef cooked in underground ovens and they were both delicious. The beef was at a Mexican wedding, where I learned that underground ovens have long been a tradition in Mexican cultures. In an attempt to give you instructions in this art, I accessed the internet. The 'Old Lahaina Luau", along with the Culinary Arts program at Maui Community College have a very entertaining and educational 30 step program for cooking your pig. There is nothing I could add to it. Just type in Imu Pig in your search slot and you'll get this and several other choices for instructions. If it sounds like too much work, go to the Luau. The food is delightful and the show, magical.

POI

I'm sure most Midwesterners think a field of corn is a beautiful sight. Vistas of rice paddies show up in many Chinese paintings. To me, one of the most beautiful agricultural sights in the world, is a Taro field. Taro fields are the birthplace of Poi. To make Poi, you boil, peel, and mash the root of the beautiful Taro plant. While Poi is, without question, an acquired taste, the nutritional value is indisputable. It has been called the most nutritious and healing plant on earth. It is easily digestible for elders and infants and has saved the lives of children so ill, they couldn't digest even mother's milk. Rich in calcium, phosphorous and vitamin B, it no doubt accounts for the dazzling teeth in the Polynesians. The early non-Polynesian settlers in the Islands sought ways to incorporate Poi into their diets in forms more familiar to them. They thickened stews and puddings with it and used it in place of flour in many bread products. Now there is a company, called The Poi Company, that use it in English muffins, bagels, biscotti, lavosh, salad dressings, cheesecakes and ice cream. Many of these items could be a boon for folks with allergies to the usual ingredients in these foods. Contact them at www.thepoicompany.com.

BOILED PEANUTS

This recipe comes with a story. My daughter (da skinny one) was at the annual rodeo in Makawao, on the island of Maui. She sat herself in the midst of a large, in every sense of the word, Hawaiian family. As the day wore on and the paniolos were roping calves, taming broncos and riding bulls, huge men were stomping, yelling approval, holding up babies and shaking the very stands with their enthusiam. All the while one of those regal, beautiful and stately Hawaiian matrons sat quietly beside my daughter, occasionly offering her a boiled peanut. The last event of the day was steer-roping. A very wary looking long horn steer ploughed into the arena with a cowboy hot on his heels. The cowboy jumped from his horse, grabbed the horns and was wrestling the animal to the ground when the steer flipped his head and sent the cowboy flying across the field. At this the Hawaiian lady jumped up and down, cheering and waving her arms. When she finally sat down again, my daughter gave her a big smile. She smiled back and said " mo bettah da cow wins."

1 pound peanuts, in the shell
2 tablespoons salt
1 teaspoon sugar
1 star anise

Soak peanuts overnight. Drain and cover with fresh water. Add salt, sugar and anise to the water. Boil for 20 minutes. Taste. If you like them softer, boil longer. Cool.

Desserts

HAUPIA

I have never been to a party of any kind in Hawaii that didn't have Haupia. Luaus, baptisms, graduations, they all serve Haupia. I think it's required. It's very easy to make if you use canned or frozen coconut milk. See facing page to make your own coconut milk.

3 cups coconut milk
½ cup cornstarch
½ cup sugar
pinch salt

In a saucepan, mix sugar and cornstarch. Stir in coconut milk. Turn the heat on low and continue stirring until thickened. Pour into square baking pan and chill until firm. Cut into squares.

Although it's not traditional, I like toasted coconut mixed with toasted almonds sprinkled on top.

Serves 8 or 10

COCONUT MILK

There are many fine brands of coconut milk on the market, canned and frozen. I have found that you pretty much get what you pay for. The least expensive brands seem to be inconsistent in both flavor and consistency. To make your own, pierce the coconuts and drain liquid into a container*. Remove and grate the coconut meat. Place in a bowl and cover it with very hot water. You will need 4 cups coconut meat to 2 cups water. Let stand for 20 minutes. Place coconut meat in double cheesecloth and squeeze to remove all the cream. To make a thicker cream, use 6 cups coconut to 2 cups water. Place in the refrigerator. A thick cream will form on the surface. Skim this off to make 2 cups thick coconut cream.

*This liquid can and should be drunk. It's nutritious and delicious once you get used to it.

TROPICAL RICE PUDDING

3 cups milk
2 eggs
¾ cup sugar
1 teaspoon vanilla
pinch salt
3 cups cooked long grain rice
½ cup shredded coconut

Beat eggs and add to milk. Add sugar, blend well, and add vanilla and salt.
Stir in rice and coconut. Pour into 2 quart baking dish. Place baking dish in pan of water and bake at 350 degrees for 50 minutes or until firm. Cool slightly and serve with Mango Creme Sauce .

Mango Creme Sauce

1 large mango, peeled and pitted
2 tablespoons sugar
1 tablespoon orange liqueur
2 tablespoons heavy cream or ½ and ½
water, if necessary

Put mango pieces into blender. Add sugar and orange liqueur. Blend until smooth. Add cream and blend just until mixed in. If the consistency is too thick, add a tablespoon of water and pulse blend until smooth.

Serves 4 to 6

MALASADAS

Malasadas, Portuguese in origin, are a very popular item in the islands. They are very much like glazed donuts. You can drizzle them with honey or sprinkle them with sugar and cinnamon but tradition requires that you shake them in a bag with just sugar.

1 cake yeast
¼ cup warm water
6 cups flour
¾ cup sugar
½ teaspoon salt
¼ cup melted butter
2 cups milk
5 large or 6 small eggs, beaten
oil for frying
sugar

Dissolve yeast in warm water. Sift flour, add eggs, butter, sugar, salt, and yeast. Mix well adding milk, a little at a time. Beat until dough is soft. Cover dough and set aside in a warm place until it doubles in bulk, 3 to 4 hours. Turn dough and allow to rise again. Drop dough by tablespoonful into hot oil, turning to brown evenly. Remove to paper towels to drain. Drop into bag of sugar and shake.

Makes 25 to 30

COCONUT MOLDS IN
RASPBERRY SAUCE

2 cups milk
2 tablespoons gelatin powder
2 cups whipped cream
¼ teaspoon salt
½ cup powdered sugar
2 cups freshly grated coconut or
1 ½ cup unsweetened dried coconut
1 cup mango or pineapple pieces, cut ¼ inch and drained

Dissolve gelatin in 2 tablespoons of the milk. Bring the rest of the milk to the boiling point and add the gelatin mixture. Stir to combine and chill. Combine salt, sugar, coconut and fruit pieces and gently fold this and the whipped cream into the gelatin and milk mixture. Place in large mold or individual molds. Chill until firm and unmold on dessert plates. If you have difficulty unmolding, dip molds into very warm water for a second or two.

Raspberry Sauce, 2 versions

1 cup raspberries
½ cup sugar
1 teaspoon cornstarch
2 tablespoons water

Mix cornstarch with water and add to berries with sugar. Cook over low to medium heat until sugar is dissolved and mixture has thickened slightly. Strain if desired.

Alternately: Heat ½ cup raspberry jam with 2 or 3 tablespoons water. Add 1 or 2 tablespoons fruit liqueur such as Apricot Brandy or Grand Marnier, if desired.

Serves 6 to 8

WON TON SURPRISES

This is one for the kids. They can even help make them. They are best right out of the frying pan but keep well for several hours. If you take them to a picnic, carry them in a paper bag to maintain their crispness.

20 won ton skins
1 small package cream cheese
½ cup berry jam, any jam you like will do*
1 egg
oil for frying
powdered sugar

Spread won ton skins on working space. Spoon 1 teaspoon each of jam and cream cheese on each skin. Beat the egg and apply to the edges of each skin. Fold skins and seal with the cheese mixture in the center. Heat oil until a drop of water spatters and fry the won tons, a few at a time. Drain on paper towels and sprinkle with powdered sugar.

Jellies are inclined to liquify when heated so pick a good thick jam.

Makes 20

OATMEAL MACAROONS

Macaroons are flourless and therefore light. They make a nice accompaniment for puddings.

1 egg white
¼ teaspoon salt
1 cup sugar
1 cup oats
¼ cup grated coconut
½ teaspoon vanilla

Beat egg white until stiff. Combine salt and sugar and slowly add to egg white while continuing to beat. Fold in vanilla, then oats and coconut. Droop by teaspoonful onto greased cookie sheet. Cook at 350 degrees for 12 minutes.

Makes about 18 cookies

PINEAPPLE MACADAMIA NUT BREAD

This can be a healthy breakfast, as well as a delicious treat.

2 ¼ cups sifted flour, half whole wheat if desired
¾ cups sugar
1 ½ teaspoon salt
3 teaspoons baking powder
½ teaspoon baking soda
1 cup shredded whole bran cereal
¾ cups macadamia nuts, chopped
1 ½ cups canned, crushed pineapple, with juice
1 beaten egg
3 tablespoons melted butter

Sift the dry ingredients together twice. Stir in the remaining ingredients and mix well. Pour into a well greased loaf pan and bake at 350 degrees for 1 ¼ hours. This bread stays moist for several days.

HAWAIIAN FRUIT TORTE

Use your favorite fruit for this or whatever is not going to keep much longer. It will get eaten this way.

1 ½ cups cookie or graham cracker crumbs, or some of both
3 tablespoons butter or margarine
dash nutmeg
fruit: mangos, bananas, pineapple, kiwi, berries, guava or?

Mix the cookie crumbs with the butter and nutmeg and press into the bottom of a shallow cake or torte pan. Cut the fruit carefully into nice shapes, the mango in wedges, the pineapple in slices, then wedges, the bananas in uniform slices etc. Layer them in circles in the pan, overlapping the layers slightly. When you are happy with your design, sprinkle the topping all over it. This will somewhat obliterate your pattern but it shows when it's cut. Bake in a 350 degree oven for 30 minutes. Good hot with ice cream!

Topping

½ cup light brown sugar
2 tablespoons butter or margarine
¼ cup flour
½ cup macadamia nuts or almonds, chopped

Blend sugar, flour and butter. Add nuts and mix.

Serves 6 to 8

PINEAPPLE BON-BONS

This is more like a candy than a dessert but it is often the perfect thing to serve with coffee after a large meal. The kids, of course, love them.

3 cups crushed pineapple, fresh or canned
3 cups sugar
1 cup Calrose or other sushi rice
Red food coloring
Powdered sugar
Macadamia nuts

Cook rice in 3 cups of water, very slowly, until soft and dry. Mash through a sieve to make a paste. combine sugar and the pineapple in a saucepan. Add the rice paste. Cook slowly, stirring constantly until the mixture becomes dry and pulls away from the side of the pan. Mix in a few drops of red food coloring, until mixture is pinkish. Spread mixture onto a cookie sheet or other flat surface and cool, then chill for 1/2 hour.
Roll into sushi-like rolls and dust with powdered sugar. Wrap in saran wrap or wax paper and chill again. To serve, slice into 1/2 inch thick rounds and top each round with 1/2 of a macadamia nut.

FUDGEY MACAROONS

This recipe is a natural for bake sales, hostess gifts, or last minute picnic preparations. They are best eaten within a day or two but can be mixed and baked in less than half an hour so make them often. This is a great 'starter' recipe for kids interested in learning to cook.

4 squares (4 ounces) unsweetened chocolate
1 can sweetened condensed milk
7 ounces dried shredded coconut
½ cup finely chopped nuts

Melt chocolate on very low heat or in a double boiler. Add the condensed milk. Stir over low heat for 10 minutes. Remove from heat and fold in coconut and nuts. Drop by teaspoonful onto a greased cookie sheet. Bake at 300 degrees for 10 minutes. Cool.

BANANA BREAD PUDDING
WITH CARAMEL SAUCE

3 thick slices day-old bread
2 tablespoons butter
3 eggs
2 cups milk
¾ cup white sugar
1 teaspoon vanilla
1 cup banana pieces

Butter bread and cut or tear into small pieces. Place in a 9 inch by 9 inch baking pan. Beat the eggs and mix with the milk, sugar, and vanilla. Cut banana in small pieces and add to milk mixture. Pour over the bread. Bake in a 325 degree oven for 45 minutes to one hour, until custard is set. A knife inserted into pudding should come out fairly dry. Cut into squares and serve with caramel sauce.

Caramel Sauce

¼ cup butter
¼ cup white sugar
¼ cup brown sugar
½ cup cream
1 teaspoon vanilla

Melt butter. Add both sugars and cook over low heat stirring until sugars dissolve. Mix in cream and add vanilla. Cool slightly.

ABOUT THE AUTHOR

Andrea Cleall has been a part-time Maui resident for over thirty years. She has watched the fish and pineapple slices be replaced at fine restaurants with exotic and wonderful food from all over the world, especially the South Pacific and Asia. She has also noticed the food in island homes has maintained an age old tradition. It has been her pleasure to gather these recipes from friends, old and new, and to add a few of her own Hawaiian favorites. Mama Annie is who the grandchildren call when they want cookies.

Other books by Mama Annie:

Island Dancers
Island Adventures
Amazing Sea Creatures
Keli's Magic Stone
Magic Maui Cookbook

INDEX

Meat and Poultry

Luaus and Hukilaus

Desserts